# CHRISTIANITY'S
# DANGEROUS MEMORY

# CHRISTIANITY'S DANGEROUS MEMORY

## A Rediscovery of
## the Revolutionary Jesus

DIARMUID O'MURCHU, MSC

*A Crossroad Book*
The Crossroad Publishing Company
New York

The Crossroad Publishing Company
www.crossroadpublishing.com

In continuation of our 200-year tradition of independent publishing,
The Crossroad Publishing Company proudly offers a variety of books
with strong, original voices and diverse perspectives. The viewpoints
expressed in our books are not necessarily those of The Crossroad Publishing Company, any of its imprints, or of its employees. No claims are
made or responsibility assumed for any health or other benefit.

Printed in the United States of America

Cataloging-in-Publication Data is available from
the Library of Congress

ISBN-13: 978-0-8245-2678-8

1  2  3  4  5  6  7  8  9  10        16  15  14  13  12  11

# Contents

# Introduction

Jesus lived dangerously! He did not fit into the conventional culture of his day. He questioned many of its core beliefs. He sought to empower the marginalized and oppressed. And he paid the ultimate price for living so dangerously.

Being the rebel that he was, the countercultural prophet, largely misunderstood in his own time and culture, it is quite amazing that he found a place in mainline history. And despite scholarly critiques of that historical context, faith in Jesus seems to be expanding, not diminishing. However, this expansive interest in the Jesus story is itself moving beyond the realm of formal religious belief.

For almost two thousand years the Christian church sought to elevate Jesus onto a patriarchal pedestal. It began in Gospel times by the group of followers known as the twelve. Some of the Church Fathers supported the elevation. Not however until the fourth century under the daring and complicitous endeavors of Constantine did it fully bloom.

Constantine rebaptized Jesus as the Pantocrator (ruler of the universe), and effectively that is how Jesus was portrayed in Christian life and doctrine for the next seventeen hundred years. Jesus became the exalted divine hero, a perfect image of the kingly God. We had come a long way from the prophetic countercultural rebel of Galilee.

## From Power to Empowerment

Biblical scholarship of the twentieth and twenty-first centuries seeks to reclaim what has been lost along the way. We have over-politicized Jesus, but also overspiritualized him. We have made him so powerful on the one hand and so "holy" on the other that his grounded incarnational connection with us has been badly strained. Subliminally, we never lost it, and today it is being retrieved in a way that brings alive once more the prophetic inspiration of foundational wisdom.

The retrieval has several concurrent dimensions. There are those who specialize in *deconstruction,* unmasking, unraveling, and in some cases demolishing the baggage that has accumulated over the centuries; much of this baggage is about power and the ways that religion — and Christianity specifically — has been used to validate and promote patriarchal power systems.

Within the scholarly world, a range of efforts is under way at *reconstruction,* ranging from the Jesus Seminar (mainly in the United States) which reduces authentic Christian source material to a minimum, in terms of what may be considered the actual words and deeds of the historical Jesus, to those favoring a strategy of *remembrance,* which claims that the written records of early Christian times should be taken as authentic for the greater part (e.g., Dunn 2003; Tilley 2008).

Next is the growing body of adult lay people reading and reflecting on their inherited faith tradition, critically questioning inherited wisdom, and particularly suspicious of the power games being played out in the ecclesiastical realm. Many have already left the church and rediscovered their Christian faith outside and beyond it; others remain attached but often in tenuous and ambiguous ways. These lay people look to the scholarly world for inspiration, but not necessarily for guidance, and they are often alienated by the heady rhetoric of academic scholarship. They also veer toward a multidisciplinary approach to religious matters and are saddened by the absence of this perspective in much academic research. The present book comes largely from this domain, populated by a growing body of questioning, questing adults.

To deconstruction, reconstruction, and remembrance, in the present work I add a fourth and final dimension: the need to incorporate the arts in our reappropriation of the Christian story. I do this exclusively in the context of *poetry.* I also believe that poetic renditions of Gospel wisdom (as outlined in my earlier work, O'Murchu 2009) stand a better chance of honoring the new adult faith-search referred to above. Poetry is a medium informed by fierce truth. It seeks to transcend the factual nature of the prosaic rendering. To one degree or another, all poetry is extraordinary, not a derision of the ordinary but an attempt at stating what prose has inadvertently omitted, subverted, or neglected. And poetry is never satisfied: it always knows there is more to be discovered and explored.

The envisaged audience for this book are *adult faith-seekers,* those who are fed up with hand-me-down doctrinal statements, those who dread change but know in their hearts there is no other authentic choice, those who have been grappling with new insights for years and now want to trust alternative wisdom, those who intuitively have long known that Christian faith is much bigger, deeper, and more challenging than churches have ever acknowledged or proclaimed. These are the kindred spirits whose yearnings I seek to honor and whose endeavor will hopefully be affirmed in the pages of this book.

# Chapter One

# Jesus and the Imperial Demise

*To resist empire-as-such we must know what we are up against. It is something inherent in civilization itself. Non-imperial civilization is something yet to be seen upon our earth.* — JOHN DOMINIC CROSSAN

*The logic of domination, violence, reward, and punishment that prevails in the everyday world is challenged and replaced by a new logic, the logic of grace, compassion, freedom.* — PETER C. HODGSON

In this opening chapter, I want to embrace the onerous and painful task of *deconstruction*. It is an attempt to clear away some of the religious rubble accumulated over time. It is a risky undertaking frequently incurring the accusation of arrogance and self-conceit. Even more precarious is the subject material being deconstructed in this book: *patriarchal power,* and the grip it holds on the Christian religion. The task has been in process for well over a hundred years, and yet a great deal remains to be accomplished.

Socialism, feminism, postmodernism, and a range of other cultural developments certainly name some of the dynamics that need to be confronted and changed. In the present work, I want to draw on a more recent research strategy known as *postcolonialism,* which — it seems to me — provides more penetrating insights into both the rise and demise of power, along with the wisdom needed to activate a more effective deconstruction. Postcolonialism is a complex subject, which I will come to later in this chapter.

5

Two sources more easily accessible to the average reader are those of Walter Brueggemann's understanding of prophetic witness and Walter Wink's analysis of the power of domination in the New Testament. Brueggemann (1978; 1986; 1993) launches us into the prophetic endeavor with the dislocating reminder that the primary task of prophetic ministry is *to criticize in order to energize.* To paraphrase Jeremiah (1:10), we must pull down before we can hope to build up; sometimes we must destroy before we can reconstruct. That is exactly what I am attempting in this opening chapter.

Brueggemann also alerts us to the difficult nature of such an undertaking. It is very much about an alternative way of being and thinking; it involves speaking truth to power and invoking alternative scenarios characterized by subversive imagination and symbolic reinterpretation (which I will attempt through the use of poetry). It involves confrontation with the numbness of death — a challenge most of us dread — recognizing and naming that which has outlived its usefulness, grieving its loss, ritualizing the letting go, and most formidable of all, laying the dead to rest. Only then has the radically new any hope of emerging from the proverbial empty tomb.

A second source that inspires these reflections is the work of Walter Wink and his analysis of the "powers" in the time of Jesus and in our time. These are the forces that dictate cultural values in our world and exert a subtle but fierce stranglehold that leaves millions disempowered and disenfranchised. Wink identifies this destructive force as an integral dimension of our major cultural institutions, a kind of corporate personality, imposing its will often ruthlessly and brutally (Wink 1998, 27–29). Wink names this force as the *Domination System,* which he describes in these words:

This overarching network of Powers is what we are calling the Domination System. It is characterized by unjust economic relations, oppressive political relations, biased race relations, patriarchal gender relations, hierarchical power relations, and the use of violence to maintain them all, . . . from the ancient Near Eastern states to the Pax Romana, to feudal Europe, to communist state capitalism, to modern market capitalism. (Wink 1998, 39)

In nations, this spirit or power is generally called "nationalism" or "patriotism." The power of nationalism tends to be intertwined with the myth of redemptive violence. In this myth, the survival and welfare of the nation become the highest earthly and heavenly good. Here, a Power is made absolute. There can be no other gods before the nation. Not only does this myth establish a patriotic religion at the heart of the state, it gives divine sanction to that nation's imperialism. The myth of redemptive violence thus serves as the spirituality of militarism. It provides divine legitimation for the suppression of poor people everywhere and the extraction of wealth from those already marginalized and oppressed (cf. Wink 1998, 56–57) — an apt description of what daily life was like in Palestine during the earthly life of Jesus.

## The Dangerous Memory

In this chapter I want to retrieve and rehabilitate Jesus as a prophetic deconstructionist. The forces named by both Brueggemann and Wink above are precisely those that Jesus sought to change and reform. He was a fierce critic of the prevailing power structures, but that dangerous Christian memory has been largely suppressed and ignored. For almost two thousand years Christians have been living in the shadows of imperial myopia. The lure of imperial power has darkened our perceptions and confused our allegiance. The culture of patriarchal codependence has indoctrinated millions into passive submission to a ruling, controlling

God, demanding tough sacrifices and merciless in punishing those who deviate in their allegiance.

In conventional Christianity, Jesus tends to be depicted as an imperial, messianic savior, who alone can save humans from their disobedience. Not surprisingly Jesus himself gets ensnared in the imperial will-to-power, becoming the sacrificial scapegoat to pacify the angry, demanding divine patriarch. Some try to rationalize the sordid deal by claiming it had something to do with *love!* Imperialism will go to great lengths to normalize and validate its barbarity.

Even the Gospel writers get caught up in the lure for power. Somehow or other, Jesus had to be a *king;* so the Gospel narratives, while denouncing Roman imperialism, nonetheless collude with various imperial deviations; many examples are cited in the compilation of the postcolonial scholars Segovia and Sugirtharajah (2009). Until it all comes home to roost in 311 C.E., when Gelarius declares Christianity to be the official religion of the Roman Empire, and his successor, Constantine, implemented the new vision with all the power he could muster. The die is cast from there on, leaving Christians with the daunting question raised by John Dominic Crossan (2007, 237): "How is it possible to be a nonviolent Christian within a violent Christianity based on a violent Christian Bible?"

## Postcolonial Critique

The Christian religion has never been at ease with its imperial trappings. Individual Christians and scholars have, time and again, questioned the fundamental foundations of their faith, leading eventually, in the late twentieth century, toward a more systematic retrieval of foundational wisdom. The impervious imperial structure — Wink's Domination System — progressively came to be seen as a human imposition, albeit one with a complex cultural history. As we peel back the accumulated layers of distortion and confusion, we realize that for long we have been creating Jesus in our own image and likeness, an idolatrous construct of an idolatrous power-addicted regime. After two thousand years of colonial imperialism, we are beginning to glimpse another Jesus — with a salvific message very different from the popular renditions that have kept Christians (and others) subdued and domesticated for centuries.

*Postcolonial studies* came to the fore in the 1970s, seeking to combat the residual effects of colonialism on peoples, cultures, and the living earth itself (Hathaway and Boff 2009). It is not simply concerned with salvaging past worlds of precolonial times, but mobilizing the wisdom to identify and transcend the trappings of power and domination that still reap so much havoc in the contemporary world. Postcolonialist thinkers recognize that many of the assumptions that underlay the "logic" of colonialism are still active forces today. By exposing and deconstructing the racist, imperialist nature of these assumptions, it is hoped that they will lose their power of persuasion and coercion.

A key goal of postcolonial theorists is clearing space for multiple voices. This is especially true of those voices that have been previously silenced by dominant ideologies, particularly from the colonial West. The critical nature of postcolonial theory entails destabilizing Western ways of thinking and perceiving, re-creating instead space for the subaltern, or marginalized groups, to speak and produce alternatives to dominant discourse. The goal entails both deconstruction and reconstruction, with the rehabilitation of empowerment as a central feature.[1]

Postcolonial theorists alert us to the widespread tendency to create binary distinctions that seek to distinguish the powerful from the powerless, but end up valorizing and reinforcing the dangerous dualistic split. It happens frequently in Gospel texts. Homi K. Bhabha feels that the postcolonial world should valorize spaces of mixing, spaces where the unfolding and evolving nature of life can be honored, including the ambiguity and untidiness that often characterize this process. This space of hybridity, he argues, offers the most profound challenge to colonialism (Bhabha 1994, 113). When applied to biblical studies, and specifically to the life of Jesus, to some this sounds like a preposterous proposal. For so long Christians have been led to believe that there can be only one authentic interpretation for one foundational truth, safeguarded by the one true church. The appeal for unity concealed disturbing power claims.

Postcolonialism is a modern attempt to speak truth to power, seeking to release once more the dangerous memory of the foundational liberating empowerment inscribed in the foundational wisdom of our Christian faith. Since the beginning of the 1990s, a growing number of biblical scholars have engaged in postcolonial reinterpretation, producing a range of key texts, one of the better known being *A Postcolonial Commentary on the New Testament Writings,* edited by Fernando F. Segovia and R. S. Sugirtharajah (2009).

## Jesus, the Deconstructionist

I am not interested in the media-hyped deconstruction of Christian faith popularized by writers like Richard Dawkins and Christopher Jenkins, who, despite, huge media exposure, do not undermine Christian faith; to the contrary, they often evoke a fresh curiosity about it. My concern is the Jesus who embraced deconstruction as a central strategy of his life and mission. Scripture scholars — even to this day — tend to be people of religious affiliation, often with an expectation of accountability to the religious institution or organization that mandated their scholarship in the first place. This conditioning tends to influence and color their assumptions, expectations, and perceptions.

In mainline scholarship, Jesus is presumed to be a person of middle-class respectability, of authoritative male demeanor, and a loyal follower of his inherited Jewish faith. As a social scientist, it puzzles me how even a cursory reading of the Gospels could lead to these conclusions. It is even more baffling how these claims can be seen to stand up to more rigorous exegesis and discernment of biblical wisdom. I suspect there is a fundamental deviation going right through so much of our inherited wisdom: *the lure of patriarchal power.* Only when that is named, unmasked, and dethroned — as I believe Jesus set out to do — do we stand any realistic hope of becoming once more a prophetic people of the dangerous memory that can liberate fresh life and meaning.

What did Jesus seek to deconstruct? The answer is available in Wink's definition of the Domination System:

- imperial power of every type;
- the violence needed to safeguard and uphold such power;
- the unjust economic relations ensuing from such power;
- the crippling grip of irrational fear;
- slavery and oppression of every type;
- dualistic splitting between the sacred and the secular;
- human disempowerment;
- the religious validation of all the above.

How Jesus set about the task of deconstruction is what really disturbs our comfort zones: not with the respectability and power of a dominant male (the standard expectation) and certainly not with the miraculous rescue expected of a messianic hopeful. Jesus deconstructs, through subversive word and action, a strategy embedded in the great prophetic tradition of the Hebrew scriptures. The parable stories exemplify that quality of *subversiveness* in a unique way (cf. Crossan 1992; Herzog 1994; 2005). But so do the miracle stories, and we are only beginning to appropriate the prophetic empowerment in the miracle narratives of the New Testament. In this chapter, I wish to highlight the subversive empowerment of those strange stories too easily rationalized in modern spiritual literature, namely, the complex material on the dispelling of evil spirits.

As we emerge from the imposed conditioning of the past and stand with greater confidence in the light of our unfolding truth, we embrace the prophetic endeavor of speaking truth to power. It is a risky undertaking, if for no other reason that the subject material itself is complex and at times quite convoluted. The Gospels name the root problem as one of *demonic possession,* using language and concepts that are open to multiple discernment, often camouflaged beneath layers of interpretation in which we try to "normalize" or excessively spiritualize these strange experiences. The historical Jesus encountered this sinister darkness in the confrontation with evil spirits, and by adopting the archetypal images of Satan and Beelzebul he challenged the people of his day — and ours — to confront and engage the demonic power that can overwhelm and destroy (cf. Horsley 2003, 98ff.).

## Deconstructing the Demonic

The oldest known references to demonic possession are from the Sumerians, who believed that all diseases of the body and mind were caused by "sickness demons" called *gidim* or *gid-dim.* The priests, who practiced exorcisms in these nations, were called sorcerers, as distinct from physicians who applied bandages and salves. Many cuneiform tablets contain prayers to certain gods asking for protection from demons, while others ask the gods to expel the demons that have invaded their bodies.

Shamanic cultures also believe in demon possession, and shamans perform exorcisms too; in these cultures diseases are often attributed to the presence of a vengeful spirit or (loosely termed) demon in the body of the patient. Exorcisms practiced by shamans are not so much about expelling the demon as appeasing or placating it with rites consisting of respectful rituals or sacrificial offerings.

The encounter with evil spirits in the Gospels has long been interpreted as a spiritual battle with human-like creatures that can take over one's personality, activating a range of irrational and destructive behaviors. After the development of psychology in the nineteenth and twentieth centuries, dysfunction of the mind (rather than of the physical body) was considered the key problem. In both cases exorcism was the prescribed remedy, with the inhabiting force often being personalized as one called Satan or the Devil — a concept that features only minimally in Judaism (cf. Pagels 1995).

Today we understand the phenomenon of possession rather differently, as highlighted by Rita Nakashima Brock (1992, 76ff.). Many of the people in the Gospels afflicted by evil spirits exhibit a condition remarkably similar to multiple personality disorder (MPD). We readily recognize how the human personality can be overwhelmed — quite literally taken over — by a range of forces that arise in daily life. Best known are addictive behaviors such as drugs, gambling, power, sex, and even religiosity itself. These irrational drives often leave people at the mercy of manic mood swings, wild projections, and various highly destructively psychotic behaviors.

Less public but probably more perniciously destructive are the torturous, demented conditions in which millions are forced to live because of poverty, exploitation, warfare, etc. In the face of such atrocities we admire those who show exceptional resilience, but nobody wants to record the millions who succumb — mentally and physically — ending up as beggars or refugees, or incarcerated until they meet an untimely death. This is the satanic possession that nobody wants to face or even acknowledge. And in all probability many of the possessed people we encounter in the Gospels belonged to this category: demented, disenfranchised and driven insane because of marginalization, brutality, and oppression.

Scholars such as J. J. Pilch (2000), Hugh Montefiore (2005), and Steven Davies (1995) suggest that the phenomenon of Spirit possession in the time of Jesus may be compared to what we describe today as psychotic behavior. Only advocates employing more literalist interpretation of scripture take these stories at their face value. As evidenced in certain contemporary African cultures, the people in the time of Jesus were vividly aware of spirit-power and spirit-influences all around them. Like modern indigenous peoples, they may well have had positive regard for these forces — until external factors disrupted their cultural grounding, and then a range of irrational fears came to the fore creating a set of psychosomatic conditions characterized by disassociation, mania, hysteria, psychosis, inner turmoil, a sense of being tortured, an overwhelming feeling of one's destiny being out of control. It would have felt as if an alien force had taken over their world — and their personal lives.

## Internalized Oppression

This is classical breeding ground for a phenomenon known as *internalized oppression*. People begin to internalize the cruel impact of external forces that can debilitate, disempower, and traumatize people for many years of their lives. Religion often exacerbates, rather than alleviates, this condition. People are blamed for drawing misery on themselves because of their alleged immoral behavior or because of the misdeeds (bad karma) inherited from their ancestors. People become internally confused and bewildered — even to the point of insanity.

How did Jesus deal with the culture of internalized oppression? He certainly did not moralize about it, nor did he spiritualize it either. The postcolonial scholar Benny Liew (1999) suggests that Jesus began to address it in systemic terms, and that would have been a revolutionary approach in his time, as indeed it still is. He went straight to the heart of the religious establishment itself, denouncing its accommodation of forces that were not merely evil, but downright demonic. The religious household and the personal household had been infected by the same destructive power, a force that needed to be named, unmasked, confronted, and healed. Liew (cf. Segovia and Sugirtharajah 2009, 107–8) draws a fascinating parallel between Satan's house and the ransacking of the temple:

> Note the parallels between what Jesus says "in parables" (Mark 3:23), after the accusation of his acting by Satanic authority and what he does in the temple before the other interrogation about the source of his authority. He talks about "entering Satan's house" in Mark 3:27, and we find Jesus "entering" the temple, which he later specifies as a house that originally belonged to God (Mark 11:17). He talks about driving out demons in Mark 3:23 and begins to "drive out" those who are buying and selling in the temple in Mark 11:15. He talks about ransacking Satan's goods and house in 3:27, and in 11:15–16 he is overturning furniture, and stopping the movement of any goods through the temple.

The house divided against itself is the imperial corruption that undermines and usurps the people's communal life and meaning. Their spiritual and cultural equilibrium has been disrupted; the covenantal empowerment has been eroded. And before the situation can be rectified it needs to be named and unmasked. In Brueggemann's words, the task of criticizing must precede that of energizing. However, the deconstruction initiated by Jesus is subtle and deviously subversive; prose often fails to capture what is really going on. Prosaic rendering rationalizes and explains away the true reality of oppression; poetry probes the complex, and often convoluted, dynamics that are at work. When we attend to the voice of subversive poetry, we glimpse more vividly the underlying corruption — and the power of the prophetic deconstruction:

## The House and the Temple Corrupted!

*A house divided against itself*
*And a temple that's no longer a house of prayer*
*Must cast out the demons that misconstrue*
*And money-changers must be expelled too*
*Along with the priests whose wealth accrue.*
*Beelzebul became the scapegoat*
*The one to blame for evil's promote,*
*But the demon is a legion with much systemic clout*
*More than prayer and fasting to cast the legion out.*

*The strong one's house cannot be plundered*
*Without first subduing the strong one's hand.*
*While a hand that's healed on a Sabbath day*
*By what authority our laws allay*
*And temple priests he won't obey.*
*In house and temple, there's gross disruption*
*And allegations of trumped corruption.*
*He must be possessed, his gaze deranged all round*
*With no respect at all for us on holy ground.*

*The people's mind demented with evil spirits hue*
*With the demon of possession, there oft was no way*
     *through.*
*Internalized oppression their captivated soul,*
*Bewildered by the forces that seemed out of control,*
*With little hope recovering what once they knew as whole.*
*The strong man's house in tatters,*
*They wonder now what matters.*
*As companions for empowerment plow furrows to the fore*
*And the sickness of the demons must dominate no more.*

What were the external forces? Two seem to stand out. The first, already noted, is the imperial power of Rome, with the deprivations and interferences that caused substantial disruption in people's lives, often leaving them fearful and concerned about their safety and their future. The second factor was the collusion through which Jewish and Roman authorities worked hand in glove, named by Crossan (1992, 315) as "the political dialectic between possessed individual and possessed society, between demonic microcosm and demonic macrocosm," progressively leading to a religion of violence and oppression. Instead of this religion empowering people to resolve the inner conflict, the religion reinforced the internalized oppression, leaving people with a total sense of dependency on a capricious, punitive deity.

The kind of deconstruction I am proposing is illustrated vividly in the story of the Gerasene demoniac (Mark 5:1–20; Luke 8:26–39; Matt. 8:28–34). Military language is liberally used in this narrative, suggesting a man driven insane by the brutal impact of the invading Roman forces. He may well have been robbed of his land, driven into poverty because he could not pay the excessive taxes, possibly losing his entire family in the process. Is it any wonder he has ended up in such a demented, tortured state — the raw truth of which is better accessed through poetry, as I illustrate in a previous work (O'Murchu 2009, 71–73)?

A second example of prophetic deconstruction is that of releasing a woman bound for eighteen years, as described in Luke 13:10–17. The restoration and healing took place on the Sabbath, highlighting the subversive element in the narrative. Probably the subject of moralistic gossip and denunciation for many years, she can now look her ridiculers in the eye and invite them to confront the hypocrisy and cruelty — conscious or unconscious — they exert on others. What must it have felt like for the synagogue officials to see a woman who had been bent over for eighteen years now standing straight and in the wholeness of her being? Is there a metaphorical truth here carrying a far deeper significance for empowerment than any miraculous, physical cure? Once again poetry speaks powerfully to this scenario (cf. O'Murchu 2009, 78–79).

## The End of Oppression

Jesus' preoccupation with evil forces and his clear desire to rid the world of such oppression need a more imaginative reconstruction — also suggested by Pagola (2009, 169–73). Let's not rush in with the familiar solution of exorcism, or in more recent usage, the notion of deliverance. There are several hints in the Gospels that evil spirits represent *unmet needs*. The spirits inhabit the inner empty shell caused by feelings of inferiority, unworthiness, disempowerment, torture, pain, and alienation. There is nothing in the Gospel narratives to suggest that these evil forces are the result of wrong immoral behavior; their power is garnered not from wrong things the afflicted people did, but rather from wrong things that have been done to them by the brutal forces of external oppression.

If the shrieks and tremors of the evil forces represent unmet needs, then exorcism is not the answer; dealing with the unmet needs is the answer. Exorcism is not the solution; love, compassion, healing, and empowerment are the solution. Is Jesus engaging the spirits in a process of deconstruction, preparing the ground for the reconstruction envisaged in God's new reign: the *Companionship of Empowerment*? The deconstructive task is cryptically proclaimed in the words from Luke 10:18: "I saw Satan fall like lightning from heaven" (Luke 10:18), reinforced by an even more empowering statement: "If by God's finger I drive out demons, then for you God's New Reign has arrived" (Luke 11:20).

The cryptic saying of Jesus in Luke 10:18 seems to have arisen from the report the seventy had given him concerning their power over demons. Scholars have noted the nuances in the original

Greek text: the words "I was watching" in Greek is *etheoroun*, the first-person singular in the imperfect tense, which in Greek describes a repeated or continuous action normally occurring in the past.

By contrast, the word for Satan's "falling" is the word *pesonta*, the aorist participle, active voice: "to fall; to fall to one's ruin or destruction." Putting these two verbs together in this sentence suggests that Jesus was continually observing the single action of Satan's "falling." In other words, Jesus was not saying, "I saw the definitive fall of Satan in the ancient past, when he was cast out of heaven." Rather, he was saying, "I was watching; I continually observed in the victories over his minions, the ultimate downfall of Satan."[2]

The French theorist René Girard adopts Luke's statement "I saw Satan fall . . . " as the title of one of his books (Girard 2001). Girard's life-long interest is in mimetic violence, often leading to victimization and scapegoating. How do we break this vicious cycle? For Girard, the primordial breakthrough has already happened in the life and death of the historical Jesus, who embraced the role of the scapegoat and victim, yet did not succumb to its ultimate destructibility. Even though our world grows increasingly violent, the power of the Christ-event is so great that the evils of scapegoating and sacrifice are being defeated even now. A new community, God's nonviolent kingdom, is being realized.

Girard's optimistic view is difficult to credit against a background where Christendom has so frequently espoused violent means to crush its opponents. Nonetheless he is endorsing the metaphorical, even archetypal, richness of Jesus' dream for a new and different future where the prevailing forces of evil and oppression no longer hold ultimate power. The incredulity in this claim is not in what Jesus dreamed of, but in the fact that successive generations of Christians have not taken the challenge seriously.

## A New Kind of Heroism

That brings us back to the seminal text of Luke 10:18. Jesus acclaims the fall of Satan, not so much in terms of what he himself has achieved but rather in terms of what the seventy have been able to accomplish. The deconstruction — and subsequent reconstruction — requires *a collaborative endeavor.* Divine power alone can not bring about the transformation, and neither can any form of human imperial intervention. Collaborative discipleship is the strategy for the breakthrough of the new.

In proclaiming the fall of Satan, Jesus is officially pronouncing the demise of all imperial rulerships. Power from the top down is declared redundant — and ineffective. Heroes no longer belong to the top of the pyramid but to the concentric circle where disciples mutually empower each other in a collaborative endeavor empowered by a nonviolent God. Heroism is in serving a new freedom for mutual empowerment and not in achieving personal fame and notoriety. A dangerous new dream has been set aflame.

In this newly envisaged dispensation, those formerly in bondage are set free. Crippling fear can be dispelled, and those condemned to outer darkness are invited into the light and promise of the new *shalom.* And the gifts of all must be mobilized for the new collaborative endeavor. There is still, however, one major hurdle, precisely the one the church has never come to terms with: the satanic power we attribute to God himself.

The Gospels occasionally address Jesus by royal, elevated titles: "Son of God," "Lord," "Messiah," etc. And the evil spirits address Jesus in the very same way (Mark 1:24; 5:7; Luke 4:34). What does this mean? Could it be that we are looking at subversive speech in a kind of ultimate deconstruction: those who try to keep God on the patriarchal, divine pedestal are the evil spirits, and those who collude with such honorific status (and use elevated titles) cast their lot with evil spirits rather than with authentic discipleship?

Could this be the subversive clue to the enigmatic denunciation of Peter in Matthew 16:23: "Get behind me, Satan?" Scholars tend to link the allusion to Satan with the third temptation in Matthew 4:8–10: "Away with you, Satan...." Most interpretations link the rebuke of Jesus to Peter's apparent resistance to follow Jesus into his suffering and passion. Might it not also be a counter to what is widely perceived as Peter's supreme act of faith in 16:18 ("You are the Christ...")? Is this real faith or is it Peter's petrified way of saying: "I want you to be the supreme Lord and Master of my life and of everything that exists"? Is Peter confessing and proclaiming an imperial Jesus of his own making?

Some years ago C. H. Lenski observed that Peter's noble assertion of faith might have had quite a convoluted intent beneath and behind the laudable language. The words "you are not mindful of the things of God" reveals how far off track Peter really was. The word "mindful" (Greek: *phroneis*) has to do with our "thinking" or our thought life. Can you imagine how shocked Peter must have been to have Jesus reply the way he did to Peter's well-meant urging? Peter went from the lord's "blessing" to the Lord's denunciation. At the time, he could hardly have understood what was wrong with his attempt to change the course that his friend Jesus just shared with him. He didn't realize his well-meaning statement was really a "man-centered" approach to God's plan. (cf. Lenski 1964, 642; also Spurgeon 1979, 137).

The true disciple is not called to worship God or Jesus — in any guise resembling kyriarchal lordship or imperial status. Christian discipleship invokes a countercultural stance of denunciation and renunciation of all that smacks of earthly power in any shape or form. Power is in the process of being dethroned. The pyramid is collapsed into a circle. And from within that concentric web a new counterculture of empowerment is re-visioned and reborn. It will not be about proclaiming Christ in any king-like status or structure, but rather becoming Christ to others in a collaborative reconstruction, devoid of all the trappings of earthly power and glory.

Jesus dispelled the evil spirits *because they were determined to retain imperial thrones.* They thought the unmet needs could be met by regaining lost power. Jesus envisaged another way to deal with the unmet needs: a nonviolent, *empowering deliverance from within,* a prophetic strategy that was not always welcome, as we see from the confused response of the people after the restoration of the Gerasene demoniac to health. It can be quite frightening to see wholeness restored, particularly when it has implications for how everybody must realign their perceptions and expectations. Jesus did not facilitate healing, well-being, and empowerment just for individuals. As we shall see in the next chapter, the communal, collective implications were even more daunting. With imperial power routed from the scene, it must have felt like starting all over again, a scary prospect for people who for so long were told what to do in every detail of their lives. And it cannot be like that anymore! A radical new dream is coming to birth.

We will dispense with the evil spirits when we choose to embrace the fullness of our God-given humanity in the context of God's empowering creation. After two thousand years of misguided collusion, we need to face afresh the call to discipleship: the unbinding of the strong man (Mark 3:27), the collapse of Satan like lightning, the new dispensation born out of fragility, weakness, suffering, and the Cross, yet with the paradoxical power to augment radical change and transformation. I hope this book goes some way to achieving that goal, with its dangerous memory from the past and unrivaled prospects for empowerment in the future.

# Chapter Two

# Jesus and the Paradox of Kingship

*Jesus' strategy was based on an egalitarian sharing of spiritual and material power at the most grassroots level....*
*Here, I think, is the heart of the original Jesus movement.*
— John Dominic Crossan

*Although the bloody twentieth century has invalidated talk of "building" or "bringing" the Kingdom, it is still the case that what was expected of God's reign continues to energize many of Jesus' followers, including those who follow at a distance.*
— Leander E. Keck

In the time of Jesus, kings were universally recognized as the supreme governors of the earth. Democracy as we know it today did not exist. Hierarchical leadership was the norm to which every life-form, animate and inanimate, had to be subject. And at the apex of the hierarchical pyramid was the king.

What made the system so powerful, and virtually unassailable, was its divine validation. All the great religions, dating back to Hinduism, postulated a Sky-God who governed the world in King-like fashion. God rules downward — and with a firm hand. And since nobody should question the omnipotence of the Holy One, neither should anyone disobey the king. Royal governance was absolute and unquestioned.

Within the culture, all forms of authority and governance were expected to follow this model. And in most cases they did. One key institution was that of the family unit. This is where the central values were mediated; this is where young people learned how to obey and be submissive. And this is where the culture of reward and punishment was initially cultivated.

## The System of Lordship

At the time of Jesus the family system had some peculiarities that often go unheeded. The father was the head of the family and controlled every dimension of individual and group behavior within the family unit. And since Aristotle had asserted that only males were full human beings, then only the father was fully human and therefore the only one capable of representing the divine image within the family system. His wife was "a misbegotten male" whose primary role was to beget children for the ruling male and for the governing patriarchal culture. His wife was essentially a biological organism whose primary function was reproduction. And if she did not reproduce male children her role was demonized even further. Children were regarded as property, not as human beings. Male children were held in far higher regard than females. Genealogies were recorded in terms of male descent, and rights of inheritance strongly favored the male.

In the daily lives of the citizenry, every structure was characterized by this top-down control arrangement. Elisabeth Schüssler Fiorenza (1983) calls it the kyriarchal system (from the Greek word for "Lord"). Scholars with a social-science flavor, particularly Richard Horsley, Bruce Malina, Richard Rohrbaugh, John Dominic Crossan, and Marcus Borg, highlight the culture of brokering (bargaining), relying heavily on a patron-client relationship in which the patrons held most of the power and wealth, while the clients were often condemned to a status quite similar to slavery. Marcus Borg describes the prevailing inequalities in these words:

The society was manifestly oppressive. The governing class, the top 1 percent of the population, received about fifty per cent of the wealth. The top 10 percent (the governing class plus retainers and merchants) received about two-thirds. The remaining ninety per cent (mostly peasants) produced most of the wealth, yet retained, due to taxation and land ownership by elites, only about one third of their production. (cited in Boulton 2008, 228)

In every sphere of life — education, medicine, commerce, agriculture — it was abundantly clear who was in control (exercising the right of lordship, controlling the patronage) and who was there to serve, most people being slaves. As indicated in the letter to the Colossians (3:22), slavery was considered a divine mandate.

The governing elite — both Roman and Jewish — cooperated and colluded in maintaining control. As with any tightly controlled system, there were pervasive rumblings of discontent and a threshold of rebellion. For the ordinary people, life was often tough — even brutal. Severe taxes were exacted by both Romans and Jews; working conditions were often oppressive and degrading. Thousands lived on the brink of starvation, and exploitation of local resources (e.g., land) was extensive.

Millennial aspirations also surfaced, dreams of a new world devoid of Roman imperialism. Contemporary scholars such as Sanders (1993), Meier (1991; 1994), and Wright (1996) claim that restoration eschatology flourished at the time of Jesus, leading to the conviction that God was about to intervene in human history, scatter Israel's enemies, and restore once more God's true homeland among his chosen people. Messianic hopefuls surfaced by the score. Change was in the air, and this made the authorities even more petrified. This is how Walter Wink (2002, 250) describes the mood of the times:

The world that Jesus entered was seething with human longings that showed in messianic dreams, millennial fantasies,

apocalyptic desperation, mystical revelations, suicidal nationalism, religious critique and reform, reactionary rigidity, and
a sense that time was collapsing, that the future was foreshort-
ened, that the mystery of reality was about to be revealed.
In such a milieu, the authenticity of Jesus was like a beacon
that drew all mythological motifs to itself. Incubating in the
womb of that period was God's rash gamble that humanity
might become more humane.

## The Messianic Patriarch

Jesus was only one among many. The authorities had a quick rule
of thumb to discern which messianic figures might carry a ring
of truth and which should be dismissed as fraudulent. *Did they
spring from a royal lineage?* If the answer is negative, then they
are dismissed as nonstarters. If there are traces of royal descent
it must be clearly and unambiguously established, otherwise the
messianic pretensions cannot be from God.

Both the Gospel of Matthew and the Gospel of Luke provide
lengthy genealogies for Jesus, asserting that he is definitely of
God and endowed with divine power. Now if he is of God and
endowed with divine power, then there would be a widespread
expectation that he would be like a king and would behave on
par with a king. We notice how confused the twelve become when
Jesus does not live up to such expectations.

The authorities on the one hand and the male followers of
Jesus on the other (especially the twelve) are confused by Jesus'
un-kinglike behavior. Even though he forthrightly denounces
kingship, somehow the allegation persists right to the moment
of his death, when the final charge seems to be: "He claimed to
be King of Jews." For this he was crucified, posing a perceived
threat to the authorities, Roman and Jewish alike.

The early church continued the kingly attribution, mainly
through its perception and understanding of the Resurrection.

Jesus was raised in glory, to sit at God's right hand on the heavenly throne. The ensuing language of Jesus' Resurrection, even to the present time, embodies a great deal of royal accolade. One wonders how Jesus feels about it.

Eventually the glamour of the royal heavenly throne bounced back to earth — in the fourth century, when Constantine declared Jesus to be the Pantocrator (Ruler of the Universe). This was the royal approval, the indelible seal of imperial dominance, that was to characterize Christianity for the next seventeen hundred years. It did not begin to change until the mid-twentieth century.

## Jesus the Jew

Particularly in the latter half of the twentieth century, scholars tried to reclaim the Jewish identity of Jesus. Some were simply trying to honor the fact of history: Jesus belonged to a Jewish culture and religion, a fact not always upheld in Christian scholarship. Others were claiming that Jesus was primarily concerned about the reform of Judaism, rather than seeking to establish a new religion (namely, Christianity). In the Gospels of Matthew and Luke, the link between Jesus and John the Baptist seems to reinforce the perception of Jesus being in continuity with a Jewish apocalyptic/eschatological vision that recurs in various books of the Hebrew scriptures. Some contemporary scholars emphasize the Jewish origins in an attempt to redress anti-Semitism, which (they claim) Christianity has fostered from earliest times.

Laudable though these aspirations are, they leave us in something of a double bind in dealing with the cult of power within our Christian tradition. Although many scholars claim that the Covenant is the heart and soul of the Hebrew scriptures, depicting a benign and loving God, it is the punitive, domineering God, the controlling king, the successful warrior in battle that we frequently encounter in the pages of the Hebrew scriptures. It is also a God who works primarily through powerful controlling males — from the safe distance of the cloud and the mountain, but never too close to human reality.

David Boulton (2008, 405) captures the iconic significance of this background influence when he writes:

> The historical Jesus was a first-century Jew in a Hellenized Roman empire, immersed in a monotheistic Judaism, which had absorbed Persian, Babylonian, Greek, and Roman influences but triumphantly retained its own distinctiveness. The kingdom he preached and promised was a kingdom conceived within that particular, distinctive religious and social culture, expressed (and subtly modified) in the language of that culture. His glimpse of an alternative reality, his envisioned paradise regained, was a *kingdom;* the *king* was *God.* There was no other language available to a Galilean peasant-artisan unacquainted with Philo and Plato, let alone Hume's reason and Blake's imagination.

In this important quotation, Boulton seems to be suggesting that the earthly Jesus would have used the inherited wisdom, imagery, and language of the indigenous Jewish culture. Many scholars adopt this view. While I believe it may well be true of those who wrote the Gospels, and would also have been the cultural perspective of many of Jesus' followers — including the twelve — I find myself increasingly drawn to a different understanding. Throughout the Synoptic Gospels particularly, we glimpse a countercultural, prophetic, subversive Jesus whose new world order (the Kingdom of God) transgresses and transcends not merely the Jewish religion but indeed every cultural articulation of patriarchal faith-systems. Close attention to the Jewish background is essential to comprehend certain features of the cultural context, but when it comes to the individual person of Jesus, his Jewishness may be pointing us more to what he was not, rather than to what he aspired to be.

Scholars tend to safeguard the Jewishness of Jesus on the assumption that Jesus would have been a loyal and faithful disciple of his faith. How much of this is a projection of the scholars themselves — most of whom are males mandated to become scripture scholars by their respective denominations or churches? Their own felt need for power and intellectual dominance is projected onto Jesus as a law-abiding, faithful, patriarchal Jew. But surely it is all too obvious in the Gospels, particularly the Synoptics, that Jesus rejects a great deal of his culture and religion, even to the extent — as Thomas Sheehan (1986) suggests — that Jesus, in proclaiming and inaugurating the New Reign of God, was actually trying to get rid of all formal religion.

## That Strange Phenomenon Called the Kingdom of God

Throughout the latter half of the twentieth century, scripture scholars and theologians broke through the imperial consciousness that had controlled thinking minds for much of the period of Christendom. They began to question a great deal of inherited biblical wisdom. In the case of Jesus, they began to clear away the clutter of imposed imperial conditioning, culminating in a critical reassessment of one central feature — rendered in the Gospels as the "Kingdom of God."

The word "Kingdom" denotes kingship, royal privilege, and royal power. For much of the Christian era Jesus was regarded and worshiped as a king, with all the pomp and glory of an earthly monarch — and a great deal more. Jesus was the true king, the perfect earthly icon of the supreme reigning God above the skies.

It took Christians almost two thousand years to realize that the notion of the "Kingdom of God" was not in fact an endorsement of everything that kingship represented. To the contrary, it was a phrase with a complex meaning, infused with ambiguity and paradox. Gradually scholars began to realize that Jesus used the phrase in a highly equivocal and provocative manner. Jesus challenged kingship and all its inherent values; more shocking still, he denounced it to the point of ridicule and insignificance. As one scholar (Kraybill 1990) puts it, Jesus was laying the foundations for "an upside-down Kingdom."

There was more to be unearthed — and this aspect is still under scholarly scrutiny: Jesus spoke in Aramaic and not the language of the Gospels, namely, Greek. All the parables, the Sermon on the Mount, and many of the witty, pithy sayings attributed to Jesus in the Gospels were originally spoken in Aramaic. The English words "Kingdom of God" are a direct translation from the Greek: *basileia tou theou*. Aramaic renders a somewhat different construct based on much more nuanced meanings. As I have already mentioned, one suggested rendering, which I will follow throughout this book, is "The Companionship of Empowerment" (Crossan 1997, 42; 1998, 337). It is this connotation of empowerment that Jesus was trying to convey, and quite likely this is the nuanced meaning that the hearers would have appropriated. As a translation of the Aramaic, the phrase "Kingdom of God" is not only an inadequate rendering; it may actually be a false representation of what Jesus intended.

## From Power to Empowerment

The Aramaic word for kingdom is *malkuta,* formed around the root *kut,* which carries strong connotations of empowerment: *power with* rather than *power over.* Empowerment can be facilitated by a benign patriarchal ruler: empowerment from the top down. But it seems that even this mediation of empowerment was not acceptable to Jesus. It had to be empowerment *through the process of mutuality.* The pyramid had to become a circle. Gospel empowerment was to be circular, mutual, interactive, mobilizing diverse gifts, interpersonal, and lateral. It was not to be linear in any sense. Hence the significance of the word "companionship."

A radical new prophetic endeavor was coming into being. Apparently, the disempowered masses embraced it. The powers-that-be at the time became more and more threatened. They scapegoated the empowerer. And they *crucified* him. Crucifixion was a form of Roman execution not for common criminals, or even outrageous ones, but for *subversives* who were perceived as posing a serious threat to the establishment!

It has taken Christianity almost two thousand years to catch up with Jesus as the primary disciple of the *Companionship of Empowerment*. The early church, it seems, grasped the vision — how coherently and succinctly we will probably never fully know. The primordial dream might have flourished had not Constantine usurped and compromised the vision to enhance and promote his own hunger for power. He legalized Christianity (following the wishes of his predecessor, Gelarius), paving the way for it to become the official religion of the Roman Empire toward the end of the fourth century. The greatest betrayal Christianity has ever known!

By the time of Constantine's death in 337 C.E., Christianity had become an ideology of power. The hierarchy of the day was ebullient, while others felt that the integrity of the Jesus vision had been compromised beyond recognition. In protest they fled to the desert, seeking to recapture in the nascent monastic movement something of the original purity. Meanwhile, Jesus himself had been exalted both politically and doctrinally and the Christian creed encapsulated the honorific status.

Thanks to the more penetrating and discerning scholarship of the twentieth and twenty-first centuries, we are striving to reclaim the more authentic Christ-figure of Gospel lore (cf. Boulton 2008; Crossan 2007). This task will never be complete, and we are learning to live with historical gaps and a range of unanswered questions. In a sense, the scholarly endeavor is more successful at identifying the cultural and religious baggage that needs to be discarded than at portraying an authentic Jesus story that will honor the past and inspire us for the future. Despite such limitations, the ring of truth is more transparent and appealing to vast numbers of more adult Christians today; in some cases — perhaps not surprising — such fresh insights are denounced and rejected by church authorities.

Throughout this book, I adopt the notion of the Companionship of Empowerment as the more faithful rendering of the Gospel vision and therefore the central focus for living the Christian faith in this age and in every other. In the onerous task of trying to speak truth to power, we need to expose the cult of power that prevailed at the time of Jesus, unmask its power-driven controlling dynamics, and discern what seems to be of primary significance for Jesus then and now.

## Poetic Interlude

When the disciples ask Jesus about the meaning of the Kingdom, he often answers in parables. He compares the rise of this new dispensation with homely images of seeds fermenting, a woman baking bread, or a great banquet. However, we need to note that some of those homely examples are also highly subversive, e.g., working with yeast was deemed to be ritually impure. And I suggest it is not by accident that each parable opens with the word: *"imagine!"* The awakening of imagination seems to be a crucial factor in embracing and engaging with this new empowering vision. That becomes all the more compelling when we hear it in poetry:

### Imagine the New Empowerment

*Imagine a Kingdom with no king at all,*
*Empowering companions in charge.*
*Imagine the seed, the smallest by far,*
*Producing a tree's entourage.*
*Imagine a farmer his wealth to forego*

*To purchase a treasure so rare.*
*A new dispensation explodes in our midst:*
*Imagine ... Imagine ... Imagine!*

*Imagine a vineyard with wine flowing profuse,*
*The joy of a new celebration.*
*Imagine a banquet with no one left out,*
*Disrupting the known segregation.*
*Imagine the sower with seedlings aglow,*
*A harvest to relish the nations.*
*No more malnutrition to torture the soul;*
*Imagine ... Imagine ... Imagine!*

*Imagine a woman with leaven and dough*
*The hands that make bread to sustain us.*
*Imagine a table that's open to all,*
*Where purity laws won't estrange us.*
*Imagine the workers for too long subdued,*
*The struggle for justice is reaping.*
*From the least to the greatest let everyone sing:*
*Imagine ... Imagine ... Imagine!*

*Imagine an end to the patriarch's reign,*
*Collapsing the power from on high.*
*Imagine a circle empowering within,*
*A freedom so new to employ.*
*Imagine the demons, controlling through fear,*
*No longer command the high ground.*
*A new world order can break through at last;*
*Imagine ... Imagine ... Imagine!*

*Imagine the challenge disciples embrace*
*To model the new dispensation.*
*The old bureaucratic with power at its core*
*Lies dead in the temple's ruination.*
*Imagine the courage and vision we need*

*When the tomb of our hopes has been shattered.*
*And the new voice arising has another refrain:*
*Imagine . . . Imagine . . . Imagine!*

Rightly, Johann Baptist Metz (1980) has described the new Jesus vision as *a dangerous memory,* too dangerous to be entertained in Jesus' own lifetime and even more so today. Both secular and religious forces have colluded fiercely to keep the power in place. But its credibility is wearing thin as the task of retrieval gathers greater momentum and a growing body of contemporary Christians seek a more authentic and empowering Jesus.

## The Spiritual Camouflage

For much of Christian history, Christians have usurped the vision and challenge of the Companionship of Empowerment (Kingdom of God). We tend to overspiritualize the concept, assigning it to personal spiritual growth or salvation in a world beyond. Devotional spirituality has often undermined biblical exegesis. In the case of Luke 17:21, the popular translation has been that of "the Kingdom of God is within you," whereas the alternative rendering "among you" or "in your midst" is not merely a valid alternative but the favored scholarly option since the statement is a response to a question from the Pharisees.[3] The popularity of the translation "within" makes discipleship of the Kingdom a personal, private commitment, aimed not at creating a better world here but seeking to procure for oneself eternal salvation in a life to come. In this way, the countercultural dimension of the Companionship of Empowerment has rarely been fully acknowledged.

On the scholarly front, highlighting the *eschatological* dimension became another strategy favoring an overspiritualized interpretation (see especially Meier 1991, 1994; Sanders 1993; Wright 1996). Several meanings are possible here, but the general gist is that God at some indefinite future time, through the process of divine redemption, will inaugurate a new age of hope and freedom from pain and suffering. To quote Meier (1994, 414), "The Kingdom of God was simply his special and somewhat abstract way of speaking of God himself coming in power to manifest and exercise his definitive rule in the end time." Eschatology is essentially a divine prerogative, not a human one; by radical trust in God and submission to God's plan for the world, humans can obtain the salvation freely offered by God.

Some scholars offer a more earth-based interpretation: the eschatological realization of heaven on earth, realized by God's grace, but in tandem with human effort and seeking to awaken a sense of human hope. Here the ultimate goal is a process of divine transformation embracing all created reality and not merely escaping to a world beyond. David Boulton (2008, 402ff.) adopts Stephen J. Patterson's distinction between an *apocalyptic* and a *sapiential* (wisdom) Jesus. The former is perceived to act through a violent transformation, a God of judgment and terror, forever preoccupied with routing the enemies of faith and order. The sapiential Jesus, on the other hand, champions earthly and personal transformation through justice, equality, and the fresh empowerment of all who have been oppressed and marginalized. The former is very much that of a divine rescuer acting on behalf of a passive sin-ridden humanity; the latter depicts a collaborative endeavor between God and people, with Jesus as the wise and empowering catalyst for new hope and transformation.

Time also takes on new meaning. Earthly kingship works mainly with a linear sense of time, seeking to develop the present time on the successes of the past. The Companionship of Empowerment is based on a vision inspired by the lure of the future.[4] In essence, commitment to the Companionship is about striving to make the world a better place for all God's creatures, a rediscovery of paradise where all can live in the nonviolent power of justice and love (cf. Brock and Parker 2008). It may sound utopian, but without this utopia, evolution can never advance into the greater complexity that God seems to intend for all creation. In this understanding, the new vision of empowerment is not merely about people and the human situation; it also embraces transformative challenges of global and cosmic proportions.

More than anything else discipleship in the new Companionship involves a massive shift in the understanding and appropriation of power. In the apocalyptic approach, the power is invested almost exclusively in the governing, controlling God from-on-high. Humans can be involved in that process only by submitting to the dictates and requirements of formal religion. There is little space in this dispensation for the Companionship of Empowerment. Its liberating dynamic — and its dangerous memory — has remained subverted, and that has been the case throughout most of the two thousand years of Christendom.

## Storming the Kingdom

When Jesus invited the disciples to embrace this new challenge, some hard sayings in the Gospels suggest the dangers and risks involved in such an endeavor. Such texts also highlight the dislocating nature of what was transpiring as the new vision began to take shape. One such text is Matthew 11:12 (also Luke 16:16), which reads: "From the days of John the Baptist until now the kingdom of heaven has suffered violence, and people of violence take it by force" ("and everyone enters it violently" in Luke). Scholars note the different emphasis placed by Matthew and Luke, which William Barclay suggests can be combined to give this rendering:

> Always my Kingdom will suffer violence; always savage men
> will try to break it up, and snatch it away and destroy it; and
> therefore only the one who is desperately in earnest, the one
> in whom the violence of devotion matches and defeats the

violence of persecution, will in the end enter into it. (See Barclay and Drane 2001, 9.)

Faced with such a dauntingly dangerous undertaking, the poet can assist us in discerning the deeper meaning and encourage us to embrace the suffering and misunderstandings that may ensue as we respond to the call of becoming more deeply involved.

## Storming the Kingdom!

*We talk about storming a city*
*In the lore of the battle for power.*
*But God's reign transgresses the normal*
*With meanings replete to empower.*
*Beginning with John and with Jesus,*
*The powers that were scared by their force.*
*So each met a doom full of violence*
*In a storm to muzzle their course.*

*But the new reign of enduring freedom*
*Was storming another relief,*
*Companions empowering a future*
*Bringing many an empire to grief.*
*The sick and the poor at the margins*
*Will break in no matter the cost.*
*Empowering nonviolence in freedom,*
*Till every embargo is crossed.*

*The Romans used violence to conquer,*
*What the Jews would endorse to subdue.*
*While the vision of Jesus embodied*
*A daring prophetic breakthrough.*
*Violating the norms of violence*
*With justice for peace to endure*
*And the price that we pay like the martyrs*
*Is the cost that disciples procure.*

*And the storm continues disrupting*
*All systems addicted to power*
*While companions acclaiming empowerment*
*At the threshold of eschaton's hour.*

## Retrieving the Dangerous Memory

Christian history has compromised its foundational inspiration, its primordial myth, its dangerous memory. While acknowledging that the notion of the Kingdom of God in the Gospels is a complex phenomenon that cannot be reduced to any one specific interpretation, Christianity in the future, in the interests of its authenticity and credibility, must confront inherited understandings that are clearly colored by former influences that have become increasingly problematic in our time. To the fore is the issue of power itself.

I want to outline, in a more incisive and clear way, what contemporary New Testament scholarship, along with a growing body of reflective Christians, is articulating afresh, namely, that Jesus radically distanced himself from the patriarchal power games of his day, heavily denounced them, and offered an alternative strategy for empowerment that proved threatening, even frightening, to the people of his time and still remains a major challenge for Christians today.

Resituating Jesus in this context expands every horizon related to Christian faith and life. And as we shall see in the next chapter it opens up radically new questions about how we understand the personhood of both Jesus and ourselves as Christian people. In concluding the present chapter I offer a résumé of the foundational truths I am seeking to reclaim throughout the deliberations of this book:

(a) I believe the heart and soul of Christian faith focus on the *Companionship of Empowerment* rather than on the individual person of the historical Jesus. Seek *first* the Kingdom (Matt. 6:33). Jesus serves as the primordial disciple not to be imitated or worshiped, but to serve as the wellspring and inspiration for how contemporary Christians appropriate and live out the mission of the Companionship in the contemporary world.

(b) The Companionship of Empowerment is based on a cosmic, planetary worldview far more expansive and dynamic than the prevailing three-tier worldview that seems to have been prevalent in Jesus' time and is still adopted by some religions today — despite scientific and cosmological insights to the contrary.

(c) The abuse of power, and the call to re-vision power in a radically new paradigm, is the prophetic dangerous memory of Christian faith — in its foundations and in our time too. None of the Christian churches have come to terms with this fact. Many have not even named it.

(d) The Companionship of Empowerment must not be envisaged as a program created for a specific time and place by the historical person of Jesus. Instead it should be viewed as an organic, evolutionary, open-ended system (like all systems of God's creation) to be reappropriated and revisioned in each successive generation and adapted to the changing contexts of different times and diverse cultures.

(e) Because the Companionship transcends the patriarchal compulsion to dominate and control, along with the extensive use of rational rhetoric to bolster that powerful dispensation, poetic wisdom can help to keep us focused on the alternative prophetic vision. We often glamorize the childlike simplicity of God, the Emmanuel in our midst. But as Segovia and Sugirtharajah (2009, 80) suggest, even a symbol as genteel as Emmanuel may be loaded with subversive intent.

## Emmanuel

*A countersign for Ahaz,*
*A challenge to his plot.*
*Isaiah's voice of prophecy*
*Denouncing to concoct*
*Not merely a reform,*
*Destabilizing force;*
*A system once so powerful*
*Now shattered in its course,*
*While another dispensation*
*Provides a new recourse.*

*The God who's with the people*
*Precocious like a child,*
*A countersign to kingship,*
*The Reign of God gone wild.*
*Transgressing all the boundaries*
*Redundant royal power.*
*The king in all his glory*
*Must face this dismal hour.*
*There's no more room for Empire*
*Even in the kingly tower.*

*A little child will lead them*
*Who knows what life's about.*
*Another plot unraveling*
*With a truth no one can doubt.*
*Non-violence is the strategy*
*Every child can represent.*
*To heal the wounds of warfare*
*And reconcile dissent.*
*Is this the new Jerusalem*
*With an archetypal scent?*

*To Caesar and Augustus*
*And everyone from Rome,*
*To Jewish power for brokering*
*A system now forlorn.*
*Emmanuel replacing*
*The might that rules from high,*
*Is all declared redundant*
*Through the emblem of a child?*
*God's lowly incarnation,*
*With hope we can't defy.*

## Chapter Three

# The Seductive Deception
# of a Personal Jesus

*Persons are not isolated but exist only in relation. Hence, it
is not Jesus' isolated body that is significant, but his body
interacting with other bodies. The corporate body generated
by Jesus interacting with his contemporaries and with us is
the incarnation of the Christ-gestalt.*

— PETER C. HODGSON

This book deliberately begins with an outline of the Companionship of Empowerment, described in the Gospels as the Kingdom
of God. I am striving to honor the starting-point that seems to
have been of central significance for the historical Jesus. In the
Synoptic Gospels Jesus does not invite the disciples and followers
to worship himself personally. He invites them to seek first the
Companionship of Empowerment (cf. Matt. 6:33), to work for
it, to contribute toward its development and growth, to make it
the core commitment of their faith in Jesus.

This (re)prioritizing is highlighted by Robert Funk (1996, 305)
in a frequently cited text:

Jesus pointed to something he called God's domain, something he did not create, something he did not control. I want
to discover what Jesus saw, or heard, or sensed that was
so enchanting, so mesmerizing, so challenging that it held
Jesus in its spell. And I do not want to be misled by what
the followers did: instead of looking to see what he saw, the

devoted disciples tended to stare at the pointing finger. Jesus himself should not be, must not be, the object of faith. That would be to repeat the idolatry of the first believers.

## Jesus and Human Personhood

The cause for which Jesus lived and died is greater than the individual person of Jesus. The Companionship of Empowerment cannot, and must not, be reduced to the individual personality of Jesus. Jesus is better understood as the first disciple of this radical new vision and not its exclusive embodiment. It knows no one embodiment other than the whole of God's creation.

The problematic issue here is the understanding of human personhood that prevailed at the time of Jesus, a subject virtually ignored by over 90 percent of biblical scholarship today and a stumbling block in the history of Christianity that has been neither named nor corrected.

The Gospels, particularly John's Gospel, portray Jesus as an outstanding individual, a heroic model to adopt and emulate. Two influences lead to this portrayal: patriarchy and Greek philosophy. Both features come together in the way Aristotle understood human personhood. For Aristotle a human person is defined by separation and isolation: true human personhood is separate from everything else in creation, must be unambiguously differentiated from all other (soul-less) creatures, and must be rescued from the enmeshment in the natural world that, allegedly, characterized the primitive stages of our evolution as a human species.

The human person for Aristotle is totally unique and different from every other organism. Humans stand alone and apart from everything else. Moreover, humans are characterized by one outstanding quality: *the power of reasoning,* a superior gift that relegates and controls emotion and feeling, secondary characteristics that can distort the rational truth of life. The resilience of

Aristotle's rationality can be seen in the late seventeenth century in John Locke's oft-quoted definition of a human person: "A thinking intelligent being that has reason and reflection, and can consider itself as itself, the same thinking thing, in different times and places."

Shaun Gallagher (1998, see online: *www.philosophy.ucf.edu/pi/pers.html*) provides a fine overview and an extensive bibliography on the subject of personalism. He concludes with these words:

> If there is consensus among personalists concerning the primacy and importance of the person, there is no dogma or unified doctrine that further constitutes a personalist ideology. Although the majority of personalists have been theists, there is no unified theology, or even a requirement that to be a personalist one must believe in God. There is no agreement about methods or definitions; indeed, even the definition of "personhood" remains an open question.

An open question in theory, but in fact quite a closed issue in the sense that the Aristotelian understanding enjoys an unquestioned priority in all forms of Western thought. Nobody dreams of disputing the underlying assumptions; it feels as if nobody should dare to. Jesus did dare to question this apparently unassailable truth, but Christianity has not yet caught up with the new face that Jesus sought for human personhood and seems to have embodied in his own life and praxis.

Humans are characterized by a robust uniqueness that entitles them to be masters of God's creation. They represent the robust God, ruling from beyond the sky. That God has already been declared a male ruler. Consequently, for Aristotle, males are the primary embodiment of authentic human personhood. Women are misbegotten males, and can only partially fulfill the human endeavor. Aristotle's Jesus could never be anything other than an exemplary male, exactly what the first followers also sought and the template that the evangelists adopted in writing the Gospels.

## A Person Like Jesus

The personhood of Jesus portrayed in the Gospels and endorsed throughout Christian history is a *false* Jesus. It is a caricature of Greek metaphysics, the popular hero of patriarchal mythology that early Christians subconsciously adopted and imposed upon the alternative paradigm that Jesus had embraced. That alternative vision is embodied in the Companionship of Empowerment. It gives birth to a very different understanding of human personhood.

In the Gospels, Jesus appears not to address this critical issue. In John's Gospel he is unambiguously portrayed as the faithful son of the governing superfather. I expect the Synoptic writers would endorse this portrayal as indeed would most, if not all, the male followers of Jesus' own time. Even if Jesus did speak explicitly on this relational sense of identity, the chances are that nobody would have recorded what he said. It would have been a shockingly original idea; and in poetry — which is perhaps its best medium for captivating the originality — it would go something like this:

### The "I" and the "We" Are One

*I am not the kind of person they envisaged me to be,*
*Aristotle's paradigm I don't embrace.*
*Neither hero nor messiah*
*Nor imperial pariah*
*And I never was a king divinely sent.*
*A person isolated*
*Uniquely quite inflated*
*My relational identity they oft misrepresent.*

*I am not the kind of person that Constantine would like,*
*The fancied pantocrator of his dreams.*
*The sum of my relations*
*Interactive designations*
*Provide the clues to my identity.*
*A different kind of person*
*In a radical transgression*
*My mission is relational towards another destiny.*

*I am not the kind of person in splendor isolate,*
*Forever weaving webs to reconnect.*
*Intense relationality*
*The core of my identity*
*The matrix that gives birth to every soul.*
*The "we" of my existence*
*And the "I" that claims persistence*
*Reconstituted truly in a new creative whole.*

*I am not the kind of person that fragments the Trinity,*
*Unraveling mystic union at the source.*
*The triune configuration*
*Symbolizes deep relation*
*Interpenetrating ever to connect.*
*Beyond the co-dependence*
*Of linear descendence*
*Lies the myst'ry of relationship that defines my deepest*
     *truth.*

As indicated in chapter 1, the Companionship prioritizes "power with" rather than "power over." It openly denounces all forms of patriarchal heroism, along with the separation and isolation epitomized by the king on the throne. Jesus stands in the center, not on the heights, and around him is the circular formation of relational personhood. This new way of being human arises from the sum of relationships that characterizes everything in the web of life. The core truth is often encapsulated in this phrase: *I am at all times the sum of my relationships and that's what constitutes my identity.*

Biologically, in the case of each one of us, relational personhood is mediated by my parents who facilitate my entry into life: I come into the world through a relationship, and every stage of my growth and development is made possible through the interactive, relational dynamics of life. Relationship is the divine blueprint for all life-forms, the human included, a dimension of Trinitarian theology highlighted by many scholars in the closing decades of the twentieth century and the beginning of the twenty-first (Taylor 1972; LaCugna 1991; Fox 2001; Johnson 2008).

Christian devotion and popular spirituality unambiguously assert the divinity of Jesus while consistently construing the historical Jesus in a human embodiment, widely assumed to be normative for all times and cultures. This tendency to personalize Jesus arises from religious sentiment of mixed fortunes. First is the conviction that God in Jesus embraces everything that is authentically human along with every aspiration of the human heart. Then follows an unexamined, subconscious set of projections that reduces Jesus to an Aristotelian human construct. While aspiring to be molded in the image and likeness of God, a great deal of popular Christianity is focused on molding God in our image and likeness.

Karen Armstrong (1993, 209–10) alerts Christians to this dangerous tendency to idolize Jesus and project onto him our needs, fears, and desires, depicting Jesus as one who loves what we love and hates what we hate. Such personalized faith, she suggests, is at best a stage in religious development rather than a mature appropriation of faith. A more mature articulation, embracing a more relational understanding of personhood, is evidenced in mysticism and can be detected in certain indigenous spiritualities, crudely dismissed as primitive by the advocates of formal religion.

## The Archetypal Human

Seeing the humanity of Jesus through the eyes of the divine Christ does nothing to rectify the misguided sense of the human being employed in both the current scriptures and in Christian faith generally. The divinity merely covers over and camouflages a corrupt understanding of human personhood. A more enlightened and empowering approach is to uncover the archetypal significance of the Christ figure, as embodied in the historical Jesus and lived out in the transpersonal set of relationships mediated through the Companionship of Empowerment.

For some readers these may be new concepts that need an introductory explanation. The notion of *archetypes* belongs to both anthropology and Jungian psychology. Archetypes may be described as *patterns of meaning, psychic blueprints embedded in the creative vacuum of the universe, informing field influence in the direction of growth and wholeness. Archetypes cannot be known in themselves, but they may be accessed in the imagination through myths, symbols, rituals, the arts, dreams, and poetry.*

In this definition, archetypes belong first and foremost to the cosmic creation itself, as a set of energy patterns that manifest in field influences; this is based on research of relatively recent origin, namely, the interface of physics and psychology (see Wallace 2007). Energy is itself infused with a capacity for meaning and a sense of direction toward greater coherence and complexity (see Smith 2007). Humans appropriate the archetypal wisdom, not merely because of some dynamics at work in our brains, but because our entire psychic makeup is always intimately connected with the source of our becoming as cosmic, planetary creatures.

All the great religions embody archetypal meaning and content, but it is often subverted and even corrupted by religion's favored adoption of linear thought and rational discourse, as well as a tendency to reduce everything to the perceived needs of the human, narrowly understood. Archetypes, however, exhibit a strange and powerful sense of resilience. As James Hillman (2004) and other scholars highlight, archetypes seem to have a kind of life of their own. They are particularly resistant to the controlling desires of major institutions, religions included.

For Christians the historical Jesus serves as an archetype for all that is genuinely and deeply human. In more theological language, Jesus is for us the human face of God made radiant in our midst. We must not rush to the conclusion that this means a perfect model or an icon of what we are all destined to become. As Walter Wink indicates, in a classic study on this topic (2002, 125), the archetype is about wholeness but not about perfection, as conventionally understood.

An archetype of the truly human embraces our humanity as an unfolding, evolving process rather than as a finished product. Struggle, incompleteness, getting-it-wrong, learning as we go along, are all aspects of the process. The historical Jesus, as an embodiment of archetypal wisdom, did not always get it right. Jesus made mistakes (more in chapter 9 below), thus empowering his followers not to be disempowered by their mistakes, but rather embrace them as a wisdom with the potential for new learning and deeper understanding.

Two possible false directions need to be noted at this juncture. First, the theological notion of divinity should not be seen as the goal of archetypal aspiring: the perfection to be attained at the end of the process. Walter Wink captures the idea when he writes: "Divinity is fully realized humanity. The goal of life then is not to become something we're not — divine — but to become what we truly are — human" (Wink 2002, 29ff.).

The second pitfall we need to be vigilant around is identifying the archetype with mythological models of the enduring Christ, e.g., the Egyptian Horus, the Greek Dionysus, the Roman Mithras, the Syrian/Babylonian Tammuz, the Hindu Krishna. This is the approach used by Canadian scholar Tom Harpur

(2004) on the basis of which he argues that the historical Jesus may never have existed. Jesus is merely a cultural replay of the Orisis story — re-echoing the position of H. G. Wells in the 1970s (and modified in the 1990s, after acquainting himself with new scholarship on the Q source). Following a similar line, other scholars argue that the historical existence of Jesus is of primary importance in coming to know who Jesus is for us as people of faith. I wish to suggest that the archetype is more foundational than any historical reconstruction.

## Empowering Personhood

The conventional understanding of Jesus as a person sounds warm, comforting, and reassuring but on closer examination can be oppressive, idolatrous, and regressive. It isolates the human being from the connective web of life, granting an exalted, inflated status that undermines rather than enhances more authentic ways of being human. While we might expect a prioritizing of the humanity in the personhood of Jesus, historically it is the divinity that has benefited. The deeper incarnational reality of Jesus is seen to be embedded in the divinity and not in the humanity.

A relational model of the human person is far more conducive for illuminating the uniqueness of Jesus as both human and divine. It emphasizes the wider web of belonging, with its nourishing, sustaining, and empowering potential for all life-forms. Few theologians have grappled with this new understanding as courageously and imaginatively as the American scholar Peter C. Hodgson (1989; 1994). The following quote captures his unique and original insight:

> God was "incarnate" not in the physical nature of Jesus as such, but in the gestalt that coalesced both in and around his person — with which his person did in some sense become identical, and by which, after his death, he took on a new,

> communal identity.... For Christians the person of Jesus of
> Nazareth played and continues to play a normative role in
> mediating the shape of God in history, which is the shape
> of love in freedom. Jesus' personal identity merged into that
> shape in so far as he simply was what he proclaimed and
> practiced. But Jesus' personal identity did not exhaust this
> shape which is intrinsically a communal, not an individual
> shape.... The communal shape of Spirit is the true and final
> gestalt of God in history. (Hodgson 1989, 209–10)

For Hodgson the "gestalt," embodied in and through the
communal personhood of Jesus, translates into three powerful
movements that constitute the Christian archetype: the Basileia
(Greek for "kingdom"), the Cross, and the Resurrection. The
Basileia (the Companionship of Empowerment) provides the core
strategy; the Cross becomes the enduring symbol in the struggle
and suffering-solidarity to bring about the new empowerment;
the Resurrection reinforces the communal identity now expanded
into the sphere of global transformation.

Ivone Gebara (1999, 82ff.) describes this approach as an eco-
feminist perspective, articulating an intimate sense of connection
and interdependence with every sphere of life — from subatomic
particles to the vast universe itself:

> We are fundamentally relatedness. But how can we better
> understand this primordial relatedness, which seems to be
> our constitutive grounding — to be prior to ourselves and
> to go beyond our individuality? I would like to deal with
> this in a series of steps: relatedness as a human condition;
> relatedness as an earthly condition; relatedness as an ethical
> reality; relatedness as religious experience; and relatedness
> as a cosmic condition. (84–85)

In a later work, Gebara (2002) describes relatedness as more vital
than any consciousness and can be reached only from within.

A human being is first of all a being-in-relationship, then consciousness, then personal creativity. Beyond the personal and interpersonal implications — which are revolutionary — lies a more primordial cosmic imprint, which new cosmologists like the late Thomas Berry claim to be symbolized in the curved nature of space-time itself. On closer examination, everything in creation is programmed to connect and interrelate, ingeniously described by Judy Cannato (2010) as *a field of compassion.* In the primordial Christian vision of the Gospels, the metaphorical curve is that of the Companionship of Empowerment.

Among contemporary cultures, the human grounding in relationality is nowhere made more explicit than in the primordial home from which humanity evolved in the first place, namely, Africa. Tragically, Africa is the part of our planet, and the aspect of our ancient human story, consistently condemned to negligence and oversight. The renowned African theologian John Mbiti (1990, 113) highlights the *ubuntu* principle: "I am because we are," which Cedric Mayson (2010, 124–31) identifies as the core understanding for every aspect of African life and culture. A. O. Ogbonnaya (1994) provides a fine overview of the African immersion in communitarian consciousness, its related views of God and the cosmic vision inherent to it. "Relatedness," he writes, "is not primarily between so-called rational beings. This relatedness is inclusive of the whole cosmos." (Ogbonnaya 1994, 14).

The African grounding in the relational way of being provides a cultural prototype of great age and depth; hopefully someday it will receive more dynamic scholarly attention. Tragically, it is Africa too that bears witness to some of the most destructive deviations observable in the relational web of life. Fierce tribal rivalries cost thousands of human lives every year, dictate political affiliations, and enhance the corruption of governments, leaving millions in dire poverty and often living on the verge of starvation. While, undoubtedly, Western colonialism has contributed to this tragic state of affairs, there is a shadow dimension to African communality — internalized oppression in another guise — that needs urgent attention and thorough reevaluation.

For the millions of Africans, impoverished, oppressed, and disempowered, Gospel miracle stories of raising the dead to life — sometimes dismissed as incredulous by Western scholars — exert a deep appeal, generating hope against overwhelming odds. This defiant inexplicable faith illuminates even further the liberating power of relationality and invites a metaphorical interpretation for stories like the raising of Lazarus (John 11:1–44) that otherwise elude scholarly analysis (see Moore 2009, 137–48). In poetry, the empowering liberation becomes more coherent:

## Lazarus, Come Forth!

*John's Gospel has signs with a surplus of meaning,*
*Whose truth is discerned by the heart of a seer.*

*The sign is a symbol, a truth to transcend,*
*The deadness of language and the morbid command.*
*The archetype wakens from the stupor of death,*
*Realigning life's energy in the power of the Breath.*
*In the journey of life, we're oft bound hands and feet,*
*While a stone blocks the cave, so hope can't compete.*
*The mind is bombarded with trivialized truth,*
*While the soul it is starving for wholesome pursuit.*
*Our lives drift along on a moribund trek,*
*With potential unbounded bereft like a wreck.*
*There's a Lazarus waiting in everyone's soul*
*To liberate captives, in freedom to grow.*
*Like Martha beseeching for millions entrapped,*
*Bereft of true life with their energies sapped.*
*"Come Forth" — the command from the archetype's source,*
*We all need to hear it and follow its course.*

*I have come to bring life beyond meaningless death,*
*Empowerment for justice with life on God's earth.*
*John's Gospel has signs with a surplus of meaning,*
*Whose truth is discerned by the heart of a seer.*

No sphere of life is immune from the energy of relationality. And yet as a human species we live far from the encompassing matrix. Our culture is so indoctrinated with competition, dualistic framing, adversarial conditioning, violence, and warfare. Certainly at this level, Christianity has proved to be a dismal failure. But how could it be otherwise, when most Christians have been largely unaware of the foundational challenge to serve and model the Companionship of Empowerment in and for our world?

Cultural nightmares of our time, like global warming and the horror scenes of warfare, are certainly shifting our consciousness — toward the awareness that our conventional ways of being and acting are seriously out of kilter with the wider web of life. We are beginning to understand differently from the outside, but at the inner level the conversion has scarcely begun. I use "inner" here as applied to both our collective and individual identities. We live with serious perceptual, emotional, and spiritual blocks to our true nature as relational beings. Aristotelian isolation has us firmly in its grip, and the stranglehold will not easily be broken.

Jeremy Rifkin (2009) offers one possible starting point. In a monumental work (616 pages of text), he describes how the human psyche is programmed — not for competition and violence — but for cooperation, altruism, and nonviolence (see also Keltner et al., 2010). A vast literature exists on this topic, very much in vogue since the closing decades of the twentieth century. What authenticates Rifkin's analysis, more than anything else, is the amount of experimental evidence he garners. He is not interested in collating utopian theories. His research is based on serious rational, rigorous science, bringing into focus dimensions of our humanity heavily suppressed in our rational competitive culture, but much more daunting, alerting us to dimensions of our human makeup that millions are not even aware of. And the entire vision reinforces the call to that deeper relationality envisaged in the living praxis of the Companionship of Empowerment.

Empowering personhood — whether understood in the empathic civilization described by Jeremy Rifkin in the twenty-first century, by A. O. Ogbonnaya (1994) as a long cherished value of the African continent, or further as a foundational orientation of Christian faith — remains one of the biggest and most awesome challenges facing contemporary Christianity. Without this personal and interpersonal revolution we cannot hope to do justice to the living out of the Companionship of Empowerment. And without radical commitment to the Companionship, Christianity's future credibility is in grave jeopardy.

Chapter Four

# The Dislocating Power of Queer Stories

*That the kings, property owners, and slaveowners repre-*
*sent God has been questioned by very few interpreters of*
*the parables, and it has been repeatedly accepted through-*
*out the flood of interpretations. Social-historical analysis of*
*the parable narratives should have led to a different way of*
*dealing with the parables.* — LUISE SCHOTTROFF

*Theology, with its inflated Western blocks of abstraction, has*
*lost the economy of parable. . . . So we are learning again to*
*speak God's Sophia in a mystery. . . . In a parable, the sense*
*of resolve does not solve but deepens the mystery.*
— CATHERINE KELLER

The disciples noticed that Jesus frequently invoked the notion of
the Companionship of Empowerment. Whether they would have
heard the words in the original Aramaic nuance or with the Greek
imperial intent is something we will probably never know for
sure. However, it is clear from the Gospels that they questioned
Jesus on the meaning of this new vision. They sought clarity,
probably a rational answer, maybe even a nice neat definition.

And what were they given? A story! "The Companionship of
Empowerment may be compared to a man sowing seed in the
field, a woman working leaven into the dough, workers in the
vineyard, guests at a wedding feast." All familiar images — in
fact too familiar for conceptual comfort then or for doctrinal

clarity in our time. These stories in Gospel lore are known as *the parables*.

## Parables and the Cultural Mind-shift

To this day, scholars debate whether the Gospel parables are unique to Jesus or based on precedents from the Hebrew scriptures or other sources in the oral culture of the day. The consensus seems to be that there is a distinctive uniqueness in the parables, above and beyond other narrative forms of earlier times. There is a provocative, engaging quality to these stories unmatched in more conventional storytelling. Peter C. Hodgson (1989, 210) provides a cryptic overview:

> The logic of domination, violence, reward, and punishment that prevails in the everyday world is challenged and replaced by a new logic, the logic of grace, compassion, freedom. The contents that make up this new world are familiar — banquets, wedding feasts, farms and farm workers, vineyards, royal households, merchants and stewards, noblemen and servants, public highways, law courts, the temple — but relations, values, behavior, and consequences have been set strangely askew and intensified to the point of extravagance, paradox, hyperbole.

Parables tend not to follow the neat structure of beginning, middle, and end. Instead they launch the hearer into a cultural, ethical dilemma; they stretch the horizons of meaning and possibility and often leave it to the hearer's own resources to come to terms with the shocking new insight.

Matthew 13:10–17 (Mark 4:10–12; Luke 8:9–10) must be one of the most baffling sections of the entire Gospel corpus. Jesus speaks in parables and seems to be doing so to the advantage of the in-house group. However, they do not comprehend what the

parables are about, nor does Jesus attempt to make it any easier for them. To the contrary, he seems to catapult them into a
deeper sense of ambiguity, the meaning and purpose of which is
quite unclear. Might it be a paradoxical and jolting device to
awaken their imagination and intuition in the hope that they
might then begin to grasp the deeper meanings to which they
are being exposed?

Matthew 13:10–17 provides us with an explanation of the
parabolic endeavor that ironically, and perhaps fortuitously,
leaves us without a clear-cut explanation. The text hints at the
possibility of grasping an important message from the parable
narratives, while asserting that the fuller meaning cannot be
grasped. And while hinting that the in-group (which could be the
apostles, the wider group of disciples, or some undefined others)
is granted special access to this new wisdom, paradoxically, they
are prevented from accessing the full message and its wisdom.
We're left with a baffling, confusing — and even contradictory —
explanation. Human rationality loses the plot!

Or is this the actual point of the complex passage: we are
dealing with something above and beyond rationality. Subversive
empowering speech needs a different strategy, where imagination,
intuition, and interpretative creativity are the crucial qualities.
We are encountering a cultural mind-shift, embedded in the
archetypal, prophetic wisdom of Isaiah, but born anew in the
Companionship of Empowerment, inviting adult people of faith
into a bold, fresh endeavor with few precedents in inherited
wisdom.

My hunch is that this complex passage of Matthew 13:10–17
contains crucial information, foundational insights, on the meaning and purpose of the Gospel parables. I am equally convinced
that we are unlikely to access the wisdom of this passage through
rational analysis, as is clear from many scholarly attempts. Poetry
is likely to render a more empowering breakthrough, within

intuitive hunches that speak to the heart and to the creative imagination. Take some time to sit with the following poem and see
what the Spirit within may awaken for you:

## The Parable of Enlightened Confusion

*The stories Jesus told them turned their world upside-down,*
*Bombarding every certainty they knew.*
*The boundaries were disrupted,*
*Their sacred creeds corrupted,*
*Every hope they had constructed*
*Was questioned to the core!*
*By the time the story ended,*
*Stretching meaning so distended,*
*On one truth their life depended,*
*What they'd known for long before.*

*Some disciples who were ready he called them to one side,*
*Inviting them to risk a dream come true.*
*Companions for empowerment,*
*A sacred new endowment,*
*Ready for a new announcement,*
*The breakthrough long proclaimed.*
*Those yet who cannot see it,*
*No riddles to perceive it,*
*Confused they only flee it,*
*And cling on to ancient lore.*

*The connection with Isaiah he thought might do the trick,*
*Their hist'ry might illuminate the way.*
*Unless the eye is open wide,*
*Unless the ear echoes from inside,*
*Unless the heart risks to confide,*
*You'll miss the haunting truth.*
*Like seeds that fall upon the ground,*
*Some parched and lost cannot rebound,*

*Yet much will flourish tall and sound,*
*And yield one hundred fold.*

*It's a text of ambiguity, true to parabolic lore,*
*Disrupting every certainty we hold.*
*With the scholars out of season,*
*There's another way to reason,*
*And to some it feels like treason,*
*To the powers who long control.*
*So embrace new liberation,*
*In the heart of God's creation,*
*And in storied proclamation,*
*Let the seeds of hope sprout forth.*

## Parables as Queer Stories

Aptly, the parables can be described as *queer stories*. In colloquial English, "queer" is a derogatory term designating odd or unusual, and in homophobic culture, it is a derisory term for a gay or lesbian person.[5] Fortunately, humans, being creatures of imagination, can rescue even the most sordid linguistic devices and put them at the service of more noble enterprises. In recent years, "queering" has become almost a science in its own right. We read about "queering politics," "queering religion." Some Christian theologians, like Althaus-Reid (2003), talk about "queering" God and Christ, while the Norwegian theologian Halvor Moxnes (2004) adopts insights from queer theory to explore boundary-stretching in the story of Jesus.

Queer theory, whose origins are often traced to the French philosopher Michel Foucault, is now widely regarded as a field of serious academic research (see Sullivan 2003). Although initially focused on dethroning the cultural monopoly of heterosexism, it is now used as a cultural critique against every effort at imposing a straightjacket, or monolithic understanding, whether in the sexual, social, or cultural realms. Using irony, ridicule, parody, elasticity of language itself, it transgresses culturally approved rationality, exposing inconsistencies and incongruities, particularly with regard to the abusive use of power. Instead it proffers more open-ended, fluid paradigms invoking the extensive use of imagination, intuition, and playfulness.

This is precisely what we encounter in the parables of the Gospels. Jesus is into queering on a big scale. And we need to remember that he doing so at the service of a new vision, the Companionship of Empowerment. Let's see how he goes about it by briefly examining two well-known parables, both from Luke's Gospel: the story of the good Samaritan (Luke 10:25–37) and the narrative of the woman and the leaven (Luke 13:20–21).

The story of the good Samaritan begins with a man beaten up by thugs and left half dead on the side of the road. We need to remember that the apparently innocuous phrase "half dead" had huge cultural and spiritual meaning in the time of Jesus. A person deemed to be half dead was considered ritually impure. Should one touch that person, or even come within a certain spatial distance, one would end up being ritually contaminated and would be unable to participate in a range of cultural and religious activities.

The priest and the Levite walk on the other side of the road, not because they don't care (they might well have been very caring people) but to ensure they are not ritually contaminated. The "queering" seeker begins to ask some awkward questions that the establishment would prefer one did not ask, e.g., "Where is Jesus in the story?" In all probability he is holding the person deemed to be half dead, in which case he is blatantly transgressing the laws of his own religion. Now Jesus becomes queer: he never explains why he is behaving in this way, and, perhaps more seriously, he never apologizes for the wrong he is doing. In one shocking transgressive moment, he declares redundant the norms deemed necessary for the effective functioning of his cultural and religious world.

And there is worse to come. It is obvious what the goal of the exercise is: this guy may be infringing the laws of God, and has effectively put himself outside the sacred, religious enclave, but for Jesus the Companionship of Empowerment recognizes no enclaves, and no form of ostracization. *There are no more outsiders!* Everyone is in — irrespective of their religious state or condition. Radical inclusiveness is a core value in the new Companionship. And then comes the bombshell, the queerest twist of all: the final act of inclusiveness is done by one regarded in that culture as a radical outsider, and a hated one at that.

Jews detested Samaritans. They deemed them to be the lowest of the low, beyond the pale of God and humankind. The detested outsider becomes the catalyst for a radical act of inclusion, in which no effort, time, or money is spared. At this stage the world context of the hearers is reeling; everything is spinning out of control. It is just too much to bear. In the vivid words of Cynthia Bourgeault (2008, 50): "Sometimes Jesus takes the language of paradox and riddle so far that he leaves people simply scratching their heads." It is also a perennial moment to enter the dislocating experience rather than seeking a rational theoretical explanation: "When we interpret a parable," writes Pagola (2009, 127 n.117), "the goal should not be to ex-plain it in clearer language than Jesus did, but to re-awaken the experience it provoked when Jesus first told it."

And then we witness what must have felt like insult piled upon insult: "You go and do the same" (Luke 10:37). But how can they, when it involves transgressing some of their most sacred laws and regulations? How will they live with their neighbors and friends after this? And more perplexing still, how will they relate with God from here on? It feels like nothing is too sacred to be protected anymore.

The story of the good Samaritan is inundated with poetic possibilities. In the poem that follows, I explore the inner world of the man lying at the side of the road, particularly that reflective moment when he realizes that he has been touched by a Samaritan, and all his old prejudices and fears come to the surface, only to move into a subversive vein as he begins to question the meaning of his own — and all — formal religion. An awesome moment of conversion!

## The Jericho Road Full of Questions

*Every bone in my body was aching,*
*And a gash just below my left eye*
*Left me dazed with confusion and anger,*
*One more victim as crime rates soar high!*
*I had heard many stories and warnings,*
*That road should not travel alone.*
*But I thought I was fit and impervious*
*A lesson too late to bemoan!*

*Many passed me and stared in amazement,*
*I never felt so much betrayed,*
*As I glimpsed the far priest and the Levite*
*My stomach it groaned in despair.*
*Till a guy with a donkey approached me,*
*A stranger so thoughtful and rare.*
*And he mounted me onto his donkey*
*And rushed me for medical care.*

*Next, I knew I was sleeping in comfort*
*And sustained with some food of the best.*
*But in nervous concern I queried*
*What 'twould cost me to be such a guest.*
*No worry but trust in the carer,*
*Had accounted for every expense,*
*With such care I could quickly recover*

*And no one would ask recompense.*

*But then came the shock and the quandary.*
*O dear! How it made my heart sink!*
*Compromising my whole reputation,*
*Betraying my unique Jewish rank.*
*Samaritans we always have hated,*
*For me they're the lowest of low.*
*How disgusting — he handled my body,*
*I better let nobody know!*

*But why did he do this good turn?*
*Now surely he too must have known*
*That Jews and Samaritans differ*
*And should keep far apart on their own.*
*I'm confused and unsure of my grounding,*
*I don't understand what's going on.*
*While the Jews all passed by and ignored me,*
*A Samaritan lifted my hand!*

*Who said we should hate all who differ?*
*On our own we should only rely?*
*And why is religion so righteous*
*Leaving people like me in the mire?*
*The Samaritans I still do not like them.*
*After all, I've been told that from youth.*
*But I can't trust the Jews any longer*
*'Cause I doubt if they're telling the truth.*

*And I wonder about all this religion,*
*Is it leading God's people astray?*
*When the outcast can glow in compassion*
*While the righteous pile rules to obey!*

The story began with a question, framed to catch out Jesus:
"Who is my neighbor?" They are left with an answer that does

not confirm their faith but turns it upside down in what they must have apprehended as a highly disrespectful and reckless piece of rhetoric. It is a dangerous memory they will not want to encounter too often.

There is also a degree of pastoral queering that contemporary Christians would need to heed if we stand any chance of honoring the Companionship of Empowerment in our day. In this story, as in every other parable, we never see Jesus employing a pastoral/moralistic check-list: Does this guy go the synagogue regularly? Does he pray every day? Is he in a regular marriage? Has he paid all his debts? Jesus does not seem to be interested in people's moral behavior. His primary, if not sole preoccupation seems to be the person's liberation from all forms of oppression. The plight of the nonperson seems to exceed anything to do with a call to conversion, as popularly understood.

## A Queer Bakerwoman

Women feature little in the parable stories. This raises some awkward questions, which we will review at a later stage: did Jesus himself at times fall foul of the debilitating patriarchal culture, or was this a limitation more of the evangelists rather than of Jesus himself? One of the more vivid female-based parables is that of the woman working with leaven (Luke 13:20–21; Matt. 13:33; Gospel of Thomas 96). Again, the story seems to be a response to a question seeking clarity on what the new Companionship entails.

And so Jesus describes the Companionship to be similar to a woman mixing the various elements to bake a loaf of bread, leavening and molding it into the dough for baking. Leaven is a lump of old dough in a high state of fermentation or a substance that causes dough to rise (yeast). A natural reason for leaven's negative symbolism is the idea that fermentation implies a process of corruption. In the Old Testament, leaven is generally symbolic of sin and evil. In every instance that leaven appears in the Bible, it represents evil.

According to Exodus 12, Jehovah commanded the Israelites to rigidly purge their houses of all leaven at the Passover season, and in Exodus 34:25 we are told that God prohibited any leaven from accompanying offerings of blood. Leviticus 2:11 informs us that leaven was also excluded from every offering to the Lord made by fire.

Presumably, Jesus would have known this, in which case we need to consider the possibility of subversive intent once again at work. Is Jesus totally denouncing all that the old dispensation represented, all that disempowered people because it often left them feeling guilty, unworthy, and disenfranchised? Or is this parabolic imagination at work, with Jesus provoking people into a radical shift in perception, inviting them to see good where, heretofore, they have only seen evil?

In this short cryptic story, we encounter two recurring themes on the eruption of the Kingdom into our midst — the new Companionship rising up as an empowering dynamic. First is the strange Greek word *enkrupto:* the woman in the parable takes leaven and hides it in the meal. "Hid" is translated from the Greek word *enkrupto,* from which comes the English word "encrypt." The root word, *krupto,* means "to conceal" or "to keep secret." The English term "encrypt" comes from the same source, denoting something secret, occult, mysterious, puzzling, involving the use of a code. This word is applicable particularly to messages or transmissions, in which certain letters have been encrypted or arranged according to a code, and only someone with the key to the encryption knows what the message really signifies. This process is often associated with intelligence work, spy operations, and wartime transmissions, but it also applies to any message that contains a hidden code.[6]

Once more, are we hearing echoes of the subversive undercurrents, the provocative new wisdom that is scrambling all inherited truth and can be unscrambled only with the key to a new wisdom, conferring a novel sense of power for the evolution of a new community? What an amazing story of transgressive concealment! On a purely practical level, the mixture of leaven, flour, and water must stand in a warm place, covered, while it rises. Everything in creation comes to birth through the gestating process, embodied in and facilitated by feminine empowerment. And while all this is happening, we wait vigilantly. In the vivid words of Luise Schottroff (2006, 206): "The woman lets her hands fall and waits."

The second recurring theme is that of the extravagance of the new Companionship. The quantities of flour being used — and the surplus of bread that will ensue — is way beyond the requirements of an average household. The dramatic imagery of this parable is made even more striking by the amount of flour that the woman adds the leaven to. Three cups (three-quarters of a pound) of flour is enough to make a loaf of bread large enough to feed ten or more adults. The three "measures" (Greek: *sata* = Hebrew: *seah*) that the woman uses in this parable, however, amounts to half a bushel (almost eighteen liters) or more than thirty pounds of flour. That would be enough to make at least forty large loaves or sufficient bread to feed four hundred people.

More important, most of the Jews listening to Jesus would have recognized the three measures of meal (an *ephah*) as the meal or grain offering (Lev. 2). According to Leviticus 2:5, this offering was never allowed to contain leaven. The listeners to the story would have been absolutely shocked out of their shoes to find that someone had the audacity, the blasphemy, to put leaven in a meal offering! That was not kosher! It simply was not done. Subversive speech at work once again.

This extraordinary imagery in the parable of the leaven was probably designed to impress upon the hearers that there would be a super-abundant yield in due time rather than immediately. And who is the catalyst for the empowering breakthrough? A woman! Sadly, she is unnamed, as tends to be the case in the Gospels. After two thousand years of biblical misogyny, let's rehabilitate her birthing creativity and her enduring resilience as a true disciple of the Companionship of Empowerment.

## The Woman Who Loves the Leaven

*Some call me the baker woman and Judith is my name.*
*I bake the bread of nourishment — to make their bodies*
      *grow.*
*I know they eat with relish and their eyes beam bright*
      *aglow*
*While I work away at leavening, God's Kingdom to*
      *empower*
*My vocation is for baking and leavening with flour!*

*I bake the food for sustenance, starvation I will end,*
*Abundant is creation, true justice I contend.*
*There's bread and water plenty for everyone to fend*
*While I work away at leavening, God's Kingdom to*
      *empower*
*Contesting every emperor the poor ones do devour.*

*Those like me doing the leavening are deemed to be impure*
*According to some crazy rule I no longer will endure.*
*The flour and bread are Godly gifts for everyone procure.*
*So I'll work away at leavening, God's Kingdom to empower*
*And circumvent the rhetoric that leaves my body sour.*

*I bake as well for Eucharist and celebrate its truth,*
*Aware of the injustice from the table we exclude.*
*I was there at the Last Supper — I cooked and ate the food,*
*So I'll work away at leavening, God's Kingdom to empower*
*And one day outwit the clerics of misogyny so dour.*

## Parables as Subversive Stories

Scholars have long warned of the danger of allegorizing the parables, e.g., assigning to God, or to Jesus, in a particular story, the role of the master, the landowner, or the king. Even the Gospel writers themselves have a tendency to allegorize, e.g., Matthew using the parable of the sower to depict four different states of spiritual disposition. Once more, we engage a double dynamic in these reflections: our desire to honor the archetypal empowerment, embedded in the vision of the Kingdom, while also grappling with the fact that many of Jesus' contemporaries did not grasp the fuller impact of the new vision. As we shall see in chapter 9, it appears that even the historical Jesus himself was not consistently faithful to the vision.

In a landmark book, William Herzog (1994) seeks to uncover the foundational character of the Gospel parables as stories of subversive speech. He claims that the stories were originally delivered and heard as disturbing, dislocating narratives, with open-ended outcomes. The stories served not as a rally call to live in a more moral or ethical way, but rather as an invitation to embrace a new and daring vision for empowering justice, and embarking upon risky new behaviors on behalf of all who were in any way oppressed or marginalized by imperial fiefdom.

Christian apologists have seriously undermined the subversive import of Gospel parables. And the domestication has been extensively corrosive. Take for instance the parable of the talents (Matt. 25:14–30). In the time of Jesus, a talent was a financial measurement, the equivalent of fifteen years wages for the average worker. And the indigenous culture was inherently socialistic with anybody earning credit or interest exceeding 12.5 percent deemed to be undermining the social fabric of life — hence the notion of Jubilee cancelation of all debts so that everybody reclaims their place on an equal playing field. Therefore, the man with the five talents has the equivalent of seventy-five years wages and when doubled corresponds to 150 years wages. The figures are grossly inflated to serve the impact of subversive parabolic speech.

The hero in the story — the person with the one talent — is actually the one denounced and condemned in popular Christian rhetoric wherein we tend to read the story within a capitalistic context and ironically use it to foster capitalistic competition. The very one who exposes the corruption and prophetically denounces the reckless landlord who gathers from where he has not scattered and reaps from where he has not sown, we also denounce, thus robbing the whole story of its potential for prophetic empowerment. Poetic intuition once again stands a better chance of honoring the original intent of the story as I have illustrated in a previous work (O'Murchu 2009, 86–87).

Herzog draws on the seminal insights of the Brazilian educationalist Paulo Friere (1921–97), who developed a pedagogy of the oppressed, through the stages of literacy skills, conscientization, dialogue, critical reflection — all aimed at a praxis that would procure at least the beginnings of an empowering liberation. As a learning process, the focus begins with people's experience, which is then subjected to critical reflection and the hoped-for awakening that people themselves need to become empowered to work out their own destiny. In our time, this vision also needs to embrace the ecological context: we cannot have empowered people in a disempowered creation as Hathaway and Boff (2009) illustrate so well.

The parables therefore serve a double function, well named by Walter Brueggemann in his analysis of the prophetic calling: the need to *criticize* in order to *energize*. We cannot renew dysfunctional and oppressive systems without first discerning, naming, and unmasking the inherent corruption. The guardians of powerful systems will go to great lengths to ensure this does not happen. The subversive pedagogy of criticizing in order to energize is risky business, yet without this daring, innovative endeavor civilization loses its life-blood, the creativity of the human spirit is compromised, and destructive ideologies eat way at the living fabric of creation itself.

That same subversiveness is portrayed with an enhanced potential for empowerment in the miracle stories of the Gospels (the subject of the next chapter). Craig L. Blomberg (1986) suggests that Gospel miracles (especially those about nature) yield a much richer meaning when viewed and interpreted as parables. Not many scholars have embraced what strikes me as a profound insight. Miracles can be understood as prophetic word in action, confronting the pain and deprivation of internalized oppression, subverting the crippling rhetoric of righteousness (e.g., the criticism of healing on the Sabbath), and empowering a breakthrough whereby the bondage of cruel suffering no longer has the final word.

The story of the healing of the leper in Mark 1:40–45 lends itself powerfully to this kind of interpretation, with the many issues around ritual purity, social ostracization, and personal disempowerment confronted in bold prophetic word. And in all probability the Gospel writer loses the subversive plot by recommending that final purification by the priests is necessary. It is highly unlikely that Jesus ever suggested this; in fact, it may be the very aspect of the story that evoked his righteous anger.

## Empowered through Subversive Healing

*It's the story of a leper who's once again made whole*
*While the narrative itself is rendered weak.*
*The limits of translation usurp subversive speech*
*And the healing for empowerment is covertly oblique.*
*Was Jesus moved by "pity" or the "pathos" that empowers?*
*The verb of righteous anger, the exclusion that devours.*
*The one who touched the leper himself becomes unclean.*
*As the plot begins to thicken,*
*At a pace that's sure to quicken*
*The old familiar world is shaken to the core.*

*The healing and the wholeness is amplified in scope*
*With the leper representing the millions without hope.*
*And the laws and regulations, the ritual and the code*
*Destabilized forever, leading systems to implode.*
*And did Jesus tell the leper to comply with priestly norm?*
*And the cleansing wrought by Moses to which he should*
        *conform?*
*Deprive we not the parable the author undermined.*
*The healing is symbolic,*
*The story parabolic,*
*Betray we not the prophet who had other things in mind.*

*Obeying the law of Moses would impress respected folks,*
*But subversiveness has little time for that.*
*Companions for empowerment, a much more urgent task,*
*Bringing freedom from oppression and justice that will last.*
*The town they may not enter, imperial control,*
*But the countryside's receptive to all who want to know.*
*The fertile re-awakening, with healing to empower.*
*We sow the seeds for justice*
*With healing and forgiveness,*
*Proclaiming unashamedly the power of God's new hour.*

The dangerous memory of Christianity has been seriously jeopardized. It began in a significant way with the compromises put in place by Constantine, a process that has gone largely unquestioned until relatively recent times. Now Christians face the momentous task of reclaiming that which has been subverted — tragically by the Christian churches themselves.

As I indicate in the final chapter of this book, it is highly unlikely that the reclaiming will come from within the churches; to the contrary the churches will continue to oppose, and where possible undermine the growing body of questioning, questing Christians, seeking a new and more authentic appropriation of the Companionship of Empowerment for our time. That is the greatest single challenge facing us as a Christian people living in the twenty-first century.

Both the miracles and the parables embody the dangerous memory — in many ways suppressed and subverted but with a subliminal appeal that cannot be totally muted. We have domesticated many of the parables, making them safe and congenial to the expectations of Western middle-class respectability. And we tend to interpret the miracles as supernatural acts that confirm our faith in a divine Jesus. In the present chapter I have briefly described the task of how we might retrieve the underlying subversive power of the parables. In the next chapter I seek to recover, not the supernatural magic, but the subversive liberation represented in the Gospels' miracle tradition.

# Chapter Five

# The Empowering Grace
# of Vulnerability

*Jesus launched a mission not only to heal the debilitating effects of Roman military violence and economic exploitation, but also to revitalize and rebuild the people's cultural spirit and communal vitality.* — RICHARD HORSLEY

*The biblical miracle stories point to the political implications of disease and to the social-psychic nature of much sickness. They present inclusive and sophisticated metaphors for understanding the relational nature of sickness and suffering.* — RITA NAKASHIMA BROCK

*Compassion is an empowering power, an efficacy, a blazing fierceness, rather than an interior emotion, and it has an efficacy for transformation.* — ELIZABETH JOHNSON

The parables serve as the primary stories illuminating the meaning and mission of the Companionship of Empowerment. The miracles are symbolic actions highlighting the personal and systemic transformation taking place under the auspices of the new empowering dispensation.

Alternatively, we can view parables and miracles as two expressions or articulations of the promised breakthrough. The parable of the creative story questions the prevailing assumptions, shatters the power-based rhetoric, and evokes new imaginative constructs for thought and speech. The parable of the symbolic action (miracle) conscientizes those trapped by internalized oppression and in the power of healing and compassion shows how people can be set free from the bondage of oppression.

The tendency to spiritualize the miracle stories and view them primarily as deeds of divine power undermines the significance of the social, economic, and political factors that give substance and passion to the narratives. Only when we embrace this wider disciplinary base can we access a fuller understanding of how the miracle activity of Jesus contributes proactively to the Companionship of Empowerment.

## Curing or Healing?

In this chapter I will review only those miracles related to healing and exorcism. Many of the New Testament healings allude to conditions such as fever, leprosy, epilepsy, blindness, and various forms of bodily incapacity. In first-century Palestine, illnesses generally were viewed as a consequence of having lost God's good favor. Ill health, therefore was a kind of curse and could be the result of one's parents sins as well as one's own.

People also lived with a vivid sense of the spirit-world. The spirits could be intimate and awesome as well as scary and frightening. Spirits inhabited every domain of life, dwelling within and without. They could be invoked not merely for personal benefit but for better fortune in dealing with all aspects of life and culture. As with indigenous peoples today, the benign and supportive role of the spirit-world was the primary experiential context for people in the time of Jesus. But when external circumstances were altered, especially because of political turmoil — along with social and economic instability — the spirit-world came to be seen in a negative light, taking on at times demonic and satanic significance.

Illness, pain, and suffering in the time of Jesus suggested a lack of equilibrium with the surrounding spirit-infused culture.

Sickness could be caused by an infringement of social, inter-personal norms and expectations. For instance, the norms of ritual purity led to exclusions and social labeling that would sound meaningless in the Western world today. And the biomedical approach to human illness, pain, and suffering was largely unknown in that epoch.

Medicine in the time of Jesus was predominantly herbal in nature. Often the herbal treatments were expensive, so substantial numbers of people would use natural remedies or turn to local healers (as in the case of healing witchcraft in Africa today). The healers often followed the shamanistic tradition of trance and the use of rituals, possibly using clay, water, extract from native plants, human saliva, or other body fluids, as illustrated comprehensively by the South African scholar Peter F. Craffert (2008, 245–308).

The modern concept of curing is very different from Gospel healing. If we seek to interpret Gospel stories as bringing about some kind of cure, we are missing not merely the richer personal context of what is happening, but also, more seriously, the complex socioeconomic and political influences that in all probability played a major role in the miracle stories of the New Testament.

## Jesus the Healer

I don't wish to dismiss the idea of Jesus exercising some divine supernatural power above and beyond human comprehension. If we are taking the Companionship of Empowerment seriously, however, we need to discern other options, particularly those that awaken and sustain incarnational empowerment. We are likely to be on a more authentic trajectory by viewing what Jesus is doing as a model and inspiration for what all Christians are called to be and to do. "You will do greater things than this" (John 14:12). What therefore is the exemplary empowering role that Jesus is adopting?

John Dominic Crossan has suggested that *healing* and *commensality* are the crucial ingredients for understanding the life-ministry and vision of Jesus. Steven L. Davies (1995) also prioritizes the healing, suggesting that the preaching and teaching that Christendom has clearly prioritized should be seen to be at the service of the healing and deemed to be of secondary significance compared with the empowerment that arose from the healing interventions (see also Craffert 2008, 309ff.). This sounds like an important shift of emphasis if we are to honor the primacy of the Companionship of Empowerment.

Preaching and teaching denote access to knowledge and wisdom that other people do not have. The preacher and the teacher can be in quite powerful roles, and often at a subconscious level can be nourishing their own need for power at the expense of others. In fact, teaching and preaching can be very manipulative of those at the receiving end. Understood in Gospel terms, healing and commensality (which we will review in the next chapter) serve primarily as empowering endeavors and should be prioritized if we wish to safeguard and promote the empowering tenor of the new reign of God in Christian lore.

Both the poet and the exegete, therefore, would need to emphasize this alternative sense of prioritizing, which is what is highlighted in the texts that describe the sending forth of the first apostles and disciples (Mark 6:7–13; Matt. 10:5–15; Luke 10:1–12):

## Sending Forth to Heal and Empower

> *You lead the way to the towns and the villages,*
> *Begin in the homes where a welcome is real.*
> *Look out for the sick, diminished in pain,*
> *The torture within, to the point of insane;*
> *Bring healing and wholeness for all to regain.*
> *Companions at one through empowerment.*

*Be risky and free in the task to empower*
*And rely on the Spirit of wisdom.*
*Tread light on the earth sustaining your way,*
*Just take the essentials and do not delay;*
*When you meet opposition, then courage you pray.*
*Companions at one through empowerment.*

*The home is your focus, the community base,*
*Companionship weaving, the loom of your trace.*
*Attend to their stories, their joy and their grief;*
*Gifts of hope and healing, you offer relief,*
*And the food they provide, gratefully receive.*
*Companions at one through empowerment.*

*If they do not receive you, don't argue your case,*
*Shake the dust off your feet and move on apace.*
*And those that condemn you because you empower*
*Stay inwardly grounded and do not grow sour.*
*Remember the prophets in your "kairos" hour.*
*Companions at one through empowerment.*

*Go easy on preaching and teaching as well.*
*Inflating your ego 'bove others.*
*You preach and you teach, empowering anew,*
*'Cause firstly you're healers for hope to accrue;*
*So heal and empower, God's reign to renew.*
*Companions at one through empowerment.*

*Two thousand years later, my mission's confused*
*With preachers and teachers bombastic.*
*Their rhetoric is empty, a vague hollow sound;*
*They fail to bring healing, mid the world's great wound*
*And they've badly ignored what I laid as the ground:*
*The mission of Gospel empowerment.*

## The Crippling Effects of Internalized Oppression

"It's odd," writes Thomas Moore (2009, 66), "given the emphasis in the Gospels on healing, that followers of Jesus talk so much about being saved." Even contemporary exegetes associate miracles with salvation: "Miracles are understood as symbols and partial concrete realizations of the kingdom of God, who comes to save his people Israel in the end time through the ministry of Jesus" (Meier 1994, 548).

At the time of Jesus, Palestine was under Roman rule. Politically, it was a relatively peaceful situation and economically quite stable. However, the majority of the people led rather sedentary lives and were forced to pay taxes that often left them pauperized, oppressed, and resentful. According to Herzog (2005, 52, 118, 174), the peasant population of Galilee was subject to three different forms of taxation: the tribute extracted by imperial Rome, the tribute collected by the Herods, and the tithes demanded by the high priestly houses in order to maintain the temple as well as their own power and prominence. Herzog (2005, 62) describes the ensuing dilemma:

> Peasants could not survive if they paid all their tribute, tithes, offering, and rents. They were unable to avoid Roman and Herodian tribute, since it was collected by force, but they could avoid paying their tithes to the temple, . . . using persuasion, not coercion, to collect its tithes and offerings. Galilean peasants were loyal to the temple in Jerusalem. . . . But they could not pay what they did not have. The temple authorities vilified the peasants and condemned them for not supporting the temple.

This led to a sense of spiritual ostracization and moral condemnation. Being in debt to the temple was deemed to be a rebellion against God. The peasants were declared to be impure, and the vicious cycle progressively became more oppressive, undermining spiritual and psychological well-being, thus relegating people into deepening levels of internalized oppression. Added to all this was the usurpation and sequestering of land by the invading forces, with laborers effectively becoming slaves, and when they could not even obtain slave labor, they then faced the frightening prospect of losing everything, even life itself. "Most day laborers live for about five to seven years after they lose their kinship and village networks. Their situation is truly desperate" (Herzog 2005, 149).

Thanks to a growing body of scripture scholars, with various skills and qualifications in the social sciences — Richard Horsley (2003), Bruce Malina (1996), Richard Rohrbaugh (2004), K. C. Hanson and Douglas Oakman (1998) — we are now obtaining a much more comprehensive picture of the social, political, and economic realities that prevailed in Jesus' time. We know a great deal more about the living conditions, along with the debilitating forces, from both within and without, that led not merely to serious health problems, but to a range of destructive psychosomatic conditions as people became more petrified and paralyzed by crippling fears.

Long after the lifetime of Jesus, but crucially when the Gospel of Mark was being written, the first Jewish Roman war (66–70 C.E.), culminating in the siege of Jerusalem and the destruction of the temple, left people suffering intensely, physically and spiritually. It is probably this latter wave of violence and oppression that informs much of the portrayal of people's pain and anguish outlined by the evangelists rather than anything during the actual lifetime of the historical Jesus. Although the violence and persecution of open warfare did not prevail in the time of Jesus, it seems that people still bore the heavy brunt of a persistent oppression that ate away at their self-confidence and general well-being, often ensuing in trauma of body, mind, and spirit.

Consequently, the crucial issue in several of the miracle stories seems to be that of *internalized oppression* (see Brock 1992, 77ff.). Condemned to brutality, slavery, and various forces of oppression, forever struggling to eke out a living, and in some cases, barely able to survive on a daily basis, ordinary people had little choice but to grin and bear it and make the best of a bad lot. In such circumstances we admire people's innate resilience, their ability to rally together and keep hope alive. What we do not see — and it may become visible only years later (or in a range of cultural projections of abusive power) — is how people have internalized the intense suffering. They learn to grin and bear it but in that process are causing deep internal damage that at some stage is likely to be manifest in sickness, bodily deformity, or mental instability.

What has been internally repressed — not deliberately or consciously done — eventually has to come out in some shape or form. Today, psychotherapy aims at bringing such painful material to consciousness, and once it has been made conscious then various options for healing can be explored. Ritual of various types can also aid the healing process. A contemporary example of internalized oppression is that of sexual abuse, the awareness of which can be triggered by life's circumstances years after the abuse occurred. More complex examples are those of political significance like that of Zimbabwe, where Robert Mugabe and his cronies, who one time championed the expulsion of the external oppressor (namely, the British), failed to acknowledge how they had internalized that same oppression. In time, that internalized oppression became the subconscious driving force that plummeted a once well-to-do country into abysmal poverty and political corruption.

Internalized oppression is the central feature of many of the healing stories — and exorcisms — in the Gospels. Internal darkness, shattered spirits, and demented minds cannot be understood by medical criteria of the twenty-first century. The critical issues are much more complex, leaving the afflicted with psychosomatic liabilities that cannot be understood by those unacquainted with the systemic forces that prevailed at the time. Let's look at two examples.

## Internalized Oppression:
## Political and Systemic

The story of the Gerasene demoniac (Mark 5:1–20) is one of the most vivid Gospel narratives. The story is peppered with military language, with the central focus on "legion," a unit comprising six thousand Roman soldiers; the term *agele,* which the writer uses for a "herd" of pigs, is often used to denote a gaggle of new recruits for the military; the Greek term *epetrepsen* ("he dismissed them") echoes a military command; and the pigs' charge (*ormesen*) into the lake sounds like a military attack — all of which gives us a vital clue to the likely context.[7] It might well be that this was a man who had lost everything — land, home, family, future prospects — and either because of involvement in peasant revolt against Roman rule or by sheer ill luck fell foul of the worst fortune of the imperial system. To use modern jargon, it drove him insane in the end.

The story may have nothing at all to do with demon possession as understood in specifically religious terms. By adopting such an exclusive religious context, we run the risk of subverting the story's foundational truth and, more seriously, the capacity for empowerment that is born out of such an atrocious tale.

The encounter between Jesus and the tormented man is not merely a case study of divine power miraculously overcoming the demonic forces that had entrapped the man and consigned him to the tombs. The story symbolizes the confrontation of God's Kingdom, come alive anew in the life and ministry of Jesus, with the violent imperial power of Rome's Kingdom. In speaking truth to Roman power, Jesus is not merely restoring a human being to sanity and dignity; he is also prophetically denouncing the power system that had so disempowered him in the first place.

This is also a useful application of the new understanding of *person* outlined in chapter 3 above. The demented sense of personhood that afflicts the man is not merely the result of personal immoral behavior; he may in fact have been a very good living man. Rather the key issue seems to be the retardation of his personality because of the systemic forces that corrupted his inner integrity, seeking to destroy his life in order to exert power over him and over his country. Rita N. Brock (1992, 79) states it quite forthrightly: "Possession is not the result of personal sin and cannot be healed by private penance. The possession comes from relationships lived under the deceptions of unilateral power."

The "sum of his relationships" became totally distorted, and his life began to fall apart under the cruel weight of brutal oppression. Jesus, the empowering healer, comes to his rescue, not necessarily through some supernatural intervention, but by unmasking the deviant forces, naming and denouncing them, and restoring something of the inner psychic balance through which he could become whole again — a process that may have taken weeks, months, or years.

The inner power through which Jesus became the catalyst for transformation and healing will be explored later in this chapter, after I have briefly reviewed another miracle story.

## Internalized Oppression: Gendered and Systemic

Following the story of the Gerasene demoniac, Mark combines two stories related to women (Mark 5:21–43). We begin with the daughter of Jairus, described by the writer as being at the point of death. Before Jesus gets to the house, he is intercepted by the woman with the hemorrhage, after which he goes to the house where we are told that the girl is dead, and Jesus restores her to life.

Many years ago, Elisabeth Schüssler Fiorenza suggested that a metaphorical interpretation of this story is likely to be far more liberating and empowering than a literal analysis (cf. Brock 1992, 82ff.). The play on the figure twelve is highly suggestive not merely to transcend a literalist interpretation, but as an imaginative entry point that evokes a more metaphorical interpretation with enormous potential for liberation and empowerment. In the historical context, a girl of twelve years old is assumed to have started menstruating, a hint that she is approaching an age when she can be betrothed to a male partner and in due course married to him. And marriage in this case signifies above all else the procreation of new life. The young woman is seen to be first and foremost a biological organism whose primary function is to co-produce children to the advantage of her male partner.

Everything associated with her coming of age, everything unique and wonderful about her in God's plan — her femininity, fertility, sexuality — is effectively demonized by projecting her into the functional role of a biological reproducer. Moreover, because of the regulations of ritual purity, every time she is menstruating, she is deemed to be ritually impure and must stay apart even within her own home, where, for instance, she will not be allowed to come to the family table to eat. In terms of God's creativity awakening in her, she is being treated as a nobody; in a metaphorical and surreal sense she is the equivalent of a dead person.

So did Jesus call her back to life literally or metaphorically? Perhaps the throwaway line at the end of the story helps us toward the more authentic answer: "Go and give her something to eat" (Mark 5:43). Is this a loaded prophetic statement in which the subversive Jesus is once more transgressing and transcending all the laws of ritual purity — and suggesting that her parents should do the same — by bringing her to the table although she is menstruating? Calling her back to life is a subversive challenge to her parents — and to the entire culture — to stop treating her like a dead person, and embrace fully everything that is happening in her body and in her life as a God-given endowment.

How do we discern the prophetic import of this "miracle"? Is Jesus in the power of subversive parabolic word and action forthrightly denouncing the misogynist culture and awakening empowerment, first, in the young woman herself and then inviting her family to honor what is really happening to her? And if she could speak for herself in the empowering imagination of her newfound freedom, what might she say? This is where the poet comes to our service, with a subversive voice prose can rarely accommodate.

In the final verse of the poem, I stretch the possible symbolic significance of her age and her gender. In some ancient myths, thirteen is the sacred number of the Great Earth Mother Goddess. Having reached her twelfth birthday the young woman is now approaching thirteen. In mythological terms, her significance and magnificence is even more sublime.

## The Daughter of Jairus Approaching Thirteen

*I'm known as the daughter of Jairus,*
*Please call me Rebecca by name*
*And my mother is never referred to,*
*Condemned in anonymous fame.*
*Well let's get priorities sorted*
*In a culture with so much distorted;*
*With women's uniqueness aborted,*
*In the name of divine platitude.*
*To bring me back to life in the Gospels —*
*Is a farce I'll no longer endure.*
*I never was dead in the first place except in the patriarch's*
    *lore.*

*At twelve years of age we young women, our bodies erotic*
　　*exult,*
*And we shed what is crimson and wholesome, our*
　　*breakthrough into the adult.*
*In the eyes of the dominant culture,*
*With the stare of a hot phallic vulture,*
*Reproducing with hope for the future*
*In the name of divine platitude.*
*It's only biology matters, for women are objects of lust,*
*Except when the sons are begotten,*
*Begrudgingly we earn some trust.*

*So the Gospels are right in declaring that I am effectively*
　　*dead,*
*For everything sacred about me*
*Is condemned in this culture of dread.*
*I'm fertile and sexual embodied,*
*God's blood and new life is not sullied,*
*And my womanhood will not be buried*
*In the name of divine platitude.*
*Empowered by the message of Jesus,*
*I'll rise to my true dignity,*
*And break through misogynist silence,*
*In the dream of a new liberty.*

*There's nothing unclean in my body,*
*And no need to drench me all pure,*
*It's all in the plan of creation, a wisdom that's sure to*
　　*endure.*
*And no need to shield me from contact,*
*Please touch me and hold me as subject!*
*And get rid of the norms that impact*
*In the name of divine platitude.*
*To the family table you bring me, in the gift of the fullest*
　　*embrace*

*Even if I am menstruating, it's all in the power of God's grace.*

*And please call me by name as Rebecca,*
*A daughter of Goddess so true,*
*An archetype thirteen remembers*
*My life and my blood will renew!*

This interpretation is also reinforced by the story of the woman with the hemorrhage (Mark 5:25–34), inserted between the two passages describing the plight of the young girl. This is a literary device often used by Mark whereby the inserted story helps to throw further light on the meaning of the other narrative, which has been split into two parts. The figure of twelve occurs again, in this case probably indicating a long time, during which the woman with the hemorrhage would be the subject of marginalization, oppression, taunting, and harsh judgment ("whose sins might have caused this?").

James G. D. Dunn (2003, 882, n.316) vividly portrays her plight: "The restrictions on a woman with a discharge of blood were severe (Lev. 15:19–27); with a continuous flow of blood she would have been socially crippled, may indeed have been quarantined. In which case, her boldness in breaching a serious taboo was all the more striking."

Her treatment at the hands of doctors was also fruitless — and had proved costly as herbal treatments were usually expensive. Are we also being told that doctors refused to deal more directly with her, lest they too become ritually unclean? She hears of Jesus in the vicinity and decides she is going to seek healing from him. We are told he is surrounded by a crowd, yet she manages to get right through to him and grabs his outer garment — and she is healed!

Most commentators seem to miss the subversive twist, making this one of the most empowering stories in the entire Gospel corpus. To get to Jesus she had to elbow her way through the crowd,

thus making everybody unclean on the way. Is she doing it deliberately? Probably, yes! In the Companionship of Empowerment,
no law, nor regulation, must stand in the way. She also makes
Jesus impure, and he as a responsible male in that culture knew
exactly what he should have done: castigate her for her reckless
behavior and hand her over to the authorities for due punishment. Instead he commends her for what she has done and heals
her.

What is the nature of this healing? Perhaps nothing particularly
dramatic other than looking her straight in the eye with a gaze of
pure love and saying something like: "I know you have had this
bodily affliction for many years, but despite it you are still a fully
radiant person, sacred in your own eyes and in the eyes of God.
Get on with your life and don't let this bodily limitation impede
you anymore." It would have been the first time in her life to
have received affirmation of this nature. Perhaps that is what the
miracle is all about.

Once more, the poet may be the one best equipped to discern
the subversive empowerment that is encapsulated and released
in this story. And contrary to the silence frequently imposed
upon women in Gospel lore, let's hear the woman echo her own
newfound freedom:

## The Woman with the Hemorrhage

*'Twas awkward and painful, but worse still 'twas shameful,*
*This curse I was carrying for so many years.*
*The clergy denounced me and the doctors renounced me,*
*While young guys pronounced me a dirty old slag.*
*I never even realized a power from within.*

*To the wind I threw caution, fed up with depression*
*And broke all the rules by joining the crowd.*
*There were stories of healing which got my head reeling*
*Through the crowd I was feeling my way to the source.*

*Determined to awaken my power from within.*

*My wisdom assured me that a mere touch had cured me.*
*I clung to his garment as hard as I could.*
*His gaze it surprised me as wholeness now seized me,*
*I stood mesmerized that 'twould happen to me.*
*Enamoured and blessed by a power from within.*

*His words were not many, but his eyes were uncanny*
*Right into my heart came the gaze of true peace.*
*What a load he had lifted, what hope he had shifted,*
*And the healing he gifted I'll never forget.*
*So much was achieved through the power from within.*

*The healer that's wounded can now remain grounded*
*And undo oppression against mighty odds.*
*And you that are wounded must never be hounded*
*By people confounded inflicting your pain.*
*Like me, you can call forth the power from within.*

(Originally published in O'Murchu 2009, 152–53)

In both these stories, we note how individual persons — both women — are being empowered. However, the empowerment is not solely on a personal level. Potentially at least they are reintegrated into the Companionship of their communities — assuming of course that the community can accept them, which apparently those who evidenced the healing of the Gerasene did not want to do: they asked Jesus to leave their territory. And did they ask the healed demoniac to leave as well? Ironically, empowerment can be a scary challenge.

## Awakening the Inner Healer

As an archetypal human, Jesus is inviting us to embrace dimensions of our humanity that have been subverted, and even corrupted, by the conditioning and indoctrination of patriarchal rationalism. We are being challenged to reclaim intuition and imagination alongside our inflated and excessive rationalism. We are exhorted to engage and transform vulnerability instead of suppressing it through denial and control. We are invited to bring hearts of compassion that can soften and lubricate the rigidities of both flesh and spirit that condemn millions to cruel pain and suffering on a daily basis. We are challenged to denounce and unmask the political and social systems that fail to deliver empowerment, dignity, and meaning (cf. Pilch 2010). And we are called to be voices for justice, for all who cry out for fresh hope!

As we assume the long haul home to the true human soul, we will rediscover a range of God-given gifts whose potential for healing and wholeness Jesus alerted us to. *Healing* as exercised by Jesus is not some supernatural power that he alone possessed, but rather a deeper human endowment *that we all possess* and that God and Jesus wish to call forth in every one of us. In many cases Jesus seems to be invoking in himself, and in those he was befriending, energy realignments or even *altered states of consciousness* (Craffert 2008; Davies 1995; Montefiore 2005; Pagola 2009, 158–68). Occasionally, this may have involved trance-like behavior, as commonly practiced by shamans and shamanesses over many thousands of years.

Wiebe (2004) suggests that Jesus was using a power similar to that employed in *hypnotism,* a healing methodology known to undo long-term psychosomatic illnesses caused by early life trauma or by the petrifying effects of internalized oppression. And there are some hints in the Gospels that he may have used healing potions from plants, soil, or human saliva, practices long known to the world's indigenous peoples. In all probability, Jesus was a skilled holistic healer, employing an innate human-divine capacity, which has been subverted in our excessively rational world and which current holistic health movements are struggling to retrieve. It is sad to see a scholar like John P. Meier dismiss these holistic perspectives as speculative ideas of "nonbelievers" (Meier 1994, 727).

Of particular relevance is the suggestion that Jesus could be regarded as a shaman, a thesis eruditely outlined by South African New Testament scholar Pieter Craffert (2008).[8] Shamanism is a complex phenomenon often superficially treated in modern esoteric and new age literature. The shaman is a mystic at heart, embodying a more highly developed human-spiritual capacity for wholeness and integration — hence the frequent allusion to the shaman as healer or medicine-person. Shamans seem to be uniquely responsive to the spirit world and therefore can maximize in themselves and in others abilities of mind and spirit for healing and problem-solving. Their capacity for ritualized behavior — through symbol, dance, trance — is never an end in itself but seems to serve the wider work for healing, wholeness, and integration. Michael Harner (1980), founder of the Institute for Shamanic Studies in the USA, suggests the following five cultural characteristics of a Shaman:

+ Initiation or ritual baptism
+ Identification with the adopting spirit
+ Acquisition of the necessary ritual skills
+ Tutelage
+ Familiarity with the adopting spirit

These five features can be identified throughout the Gospels; all are reviewed in detail by Pieter F. Craffert in his scholarly tome, *The Life of a Galilean Shaman* (Craffert 2008). Jesus was baptized by John the Baptist and learned the ritual skills from John. His identification with the adopting spirit was clear via the heavenly affirmation: "This is my son in whom I am well pleased." The necessary ritual skills are formed during testing of loyalty or temptation. A birth or rebirth is part of the tutelage, and a familiarity with "the Father" was certainly present in Jesus' ministry — notably in John's Gospel. Jesus had no power until he was in contact with the Spirit. Empowered by the Spirit, he heals and accomplishes great things. He says that we too are capable of such marvels.

However, we need to remember that the Companionship of Empowerment is greater than the individual Jesus and, therefore, healing in this larger context needs to be seen to address cultural impediments and deviations as well as personal infirmities. For people to know healing in a truly empowering way, cultural systems also need to be altered and transformed. The significance of leprosy in the time of Jesus is a pertinent example. It was not a medical condition as in a contemporary understanding of medicine; it posed little or no threat to human life. It was a form of mycobacterial infection, manifested as a particular scaling of the skin, similar to psoriasis. What made it a dreaded condition was the perception that a person became ritually unclean, a victim of social and religious contagion.

And as already indicated, Gospel references to people being deaf, blind, mute, or crippled are likely to have originated as psychosomatic conditions arising from internalized oppression that may have been triggered by inadequacies in the face of religious or social pressures, abetted by the forces of imperial oppression. For Jesus, the role of forgiveness was also crucial in initiating and augmenting the healing process — frequently, it seems within the social context of debt forgiveness, forging once again interdependent links between social deprivation, political interference, and personal suffering. For empowerment to ensue — in its fuller holistic dimensions — cultural and interpersonal factors also needed redress. The dualistic division between the sacred and secular has no place in authentic Christian empowerment.

How we might employ these insights in the contemporary world is a formidable challenge. Enormous resources are absorbed in mainline medicine, yet it is disputable that we are creating a healthier people, and medicine, despite its heavy reliance on the natural environment for a vast range of pharmaceutical drugs, seems to have little interest in planetary or environmental health. A wide assortment of alternative/holistic practices flourishes in indigenous human communities and is available in the open market in developed nations (for those who can afford the costs); yet their existence and use are often the subject of derision and denunciation by mainline medicine.

The healing empowerment in the Gospel tradition tends to be overspiritualized or dismissed as a kind of primitive magic belonging to an undercivilized culture. The problem, then and now, is that we fail to employ a multidisciplinary mode of discernment to shift us toward a more holistic understanding and an appropriation relevant for our time. Our broken, violent, and traumatized world today is in urgent need of healing. Medicine makes one contribution, and an important one. However, it is only a small part of the empowerment and liberation for which millions cry out. The Gospel healing narratives — understood afresh — offer hope and promise for the brokenheartedness of our traumatized age.

# Chapter Six

# Companions Breaking Bread

*We are earthlings and Earth is where we sit at the table of the Cosmic Banquet.* — John Surette, SJ

*The table companionship of Jesus has lost its true bite and scandal. The salt has lost its taste.* — Anne Primavesi

In the last chapter, I endorsed the observation of scripture scholar John Dominic Crossan that healing and commensality be regarded as primary articulations of the Companionship of Empowerment at work in the world. Having reviewed the healing dimension, I now attend to the revolutionary experience of the open common table (commensality) and its prophetic significance in the ministry of the historical Jesus — in the original Gospel context and for our time as well.

The nourishing power of companionship is symbolized in the central component of the word itself: "pan." It is the Latin word for "bread." "Companionship" is made possible when people gather around the sharing of food. In the nourishing empowerment of the meal, friendships are formed, deepened, and reinforced. A sharing of food characterizes all our significant life-celebrations. Table fellowship is an archetypal ritual replete with personal, cultural, and spiritual significance.

Christendom has held on to the priority of the preaching and the teaching as the primary dynamics of Christian proclamation and mission because these support the power of those in charge. Healing and commensality, on the other hand, primarily denote empowerment, of the very quality that poses a huge threat for those safeguarding the right to power. The healing and commensality are core elements in the Companionship of Empowerment and deserve a more cherished status in theology and in the daily practice of our Christian faith.

## The Open Table

Every culture tends to have quite specific expectations with regard to table fellowship and employs a range of rituals related to food and its consumption. Even within the privacy of the home, there tends to be a decorum of table custom and manners that different members of the family adopt and follow. In the time of Jesus, table propriety had a strong cultural significance, elaborated by Taussig (2009). Certain foods were deemed unacceptable for certain times and places. Those participating in a meal were expected to be ritually clean; consequently a menstruating woman did not sit at the family table. Significant males were to be particularly sensitive to their place and role at the table.

We get a glimpse into the meal expectations of first-century Palestine from this quotation:

> The Pharisees regarded their tables at home as surrogates for the Lord's altar in the temple in Jerusalem, and therefore strove to maintain in their households — and among their eating companions — the state of ritual purity required of priests in temple service.... Pharisees prescribed no special prayers or unusual foods for their meals. But they did insist on eating only with those who had "undefiled hands" (Exodus 30:19–21). The Pharisees longed for the time when all Israel would live in such a state of holiness. (S. S. Bartchy in Tilley 2008, 176)

Contrary to the Christian emphasis on asceticism, with Jesus as a model for fasting, it is difficult to avoid the conclusion that

Jesus loved food and availed himself of every possible opportunity to share food with others. Quite rightly, it seems to me, John's Gospel launches the ministry of Jesus with a feast — with wine flowing abundantly and presumably no shortage of food. However we interpret the feedings of the crowds (five thousand or seven thousand), we are left in little doubt that all were well fed. There is the danger once again that in focusing on the miraculous we bypass or underestimate the subversive. And this is the explosive dynamic characterizing many meals in which Jesus participated, both as host and as guest.

For Jesus, there seems to be no doubt about the fact that the table always had to be open. Nobody, for any reason, was to be excluded. From the highways and byways all are brought in till the banquet hall is full. Prostitutes, sinners, tax-collectors, the outcasts and marginalized of every type were welcome. Not merely were they the beneficiaries of some new bold hospitality, but it seems they were the ones who had the primary right to be at table with Jesus.

Of all the deeds attributed to Jesus in the Gospels, this might well be the most revolutionary. And the intention is unambiguously clear: *radical inclusiveness for mutual empowerment.* There is no moralizing or hints of getting all these wayward people to change their lifestyles. We are encountering an ethics of care, mutuality, and empowerment, with unconditional love at its core. And neither is it some kind of patronizing reassurance, or comforting gesture, for those under the yoke of oppression. Empowering the people to outgrow oppression seems to be the subtle, subversive agenda. All of which justifies the observation made by some scripture scholars: Jesus was crucified *because of how he ate.* Poetry glows in the empowerment of this endeavor.

### When You Give a Feast (Luke 14:12–14)

*When you give a feast,*
*With a spread so impressively hosted,*

*And choice wines have all been imported,*
*And the animals have duly been slaughtered,*
*Then you need to stop and ask yourself:*
*Who're the ones you're trying to please?*

*When you give a feast,*
*With the in-laws all invited,*
*And your work-mates so delighted,*
*And the special neighbors righted,*
*Then you need to stop and ask yourself,*
*If the guest list is complete!*

*When you give a feast*
*With companions for empowerment,*
*An alternative endowment,*
*Is there room for strange comportment?*
*Then you need to stop and ask yourself*
*What the feast is all about.*

*When you give a feast,*
*Give first place to the margins,*
*To infidels and strangers,*
*To victims of all dangers.*
*Then you need to stop and ask yourself*
*Why you left them out so long.*

*When you give a feast,*
*And a brawl might cause disruption,*
*And you stand accused corruption,*
*Fingers pointing towards deception.*
*Then you need to stop and ask yourself*
*Why you've not done this before!*

*When you give a feast,*
*To honor Jesus' wisdom,*
*Open tables cause dissension,*
*No exclusion from communion.*

*Then you need to stop and ask yourself*
*If religion can survive.*

*When you give a feast*
*Where the boundaries are all broken,*
*Parabolic truth is spoken,*
*New hope is here awoken.*
*Then you need to stop and ask yourself*
*How powerful grace can be.*

## The Egalitarian Table

Scholars suggest that Jesus adopted two popular models for his table fellowship: the *friendship meal* and the *banquet*. The friendship meal is the more informal setting of the family home, where people eat in a more relaxed way without being preoccupied with public etiquette. The Last Supper might have been a friendship meal rather than a formal Passover meal (Pagola 2009, 345–46).

The many references to reclining at table suggest that Jesus was using the model of the banquet, a more formal gathering, usually for the elite of society, incorporated into Israel from the invasive Greek culture of the time. Scholars such as Dennis E. Smith (2003) and Hal Taussig (2009) provide us with extensive insight into these meals. The food sharing was interspersed not merely with conversation and social drinking, but with formal reading, discussion, and a range of recreational activities.

After the main course came the first *libation,* drinking to the health of a Greek god, but also possibly a Roman emperor (deemed to be divine). Taussig (2009) devotes considerable attention to how the early Christian communities handled this ritual, indicating that instead of a tribute to the God or the Emperor, they would have paid tribute to Jesus as the leader of the Kingdom of God (as distinct from the Kingdom of Rome). Now we are beginning to glimpse the political, economic, cultural, and subversive characteristics of the early Christian meals — probably going right back to the time of Jesus himself.

The meals may also have provided the occasion for healing empowerment to take place. People began to dream of a new and more hope-filled future. This would have encouraged them to become proactive in their resistance, not merely to foreign imperialism, but to the oppressive nature of many of their own Jewish laws and regulations (e.g., the Sabbath observance). The commensality pioneered by Jesus was a ritual loaded with empowering intent. Assuredly, wisdom was justified in her deeds (Matt. 11:19; Luke 7:35; cf. Proverbs 9:1–6).

## Take, Eat, and Drink

Christian memory recalls one special meal, known as the Last Supper, and relegates all the rest to relative unimportance. This may well be one of the most deviant distortions we have inherited as a Christian people. The Last Supper is portrayed as an eminently significant meal which Jesus shared only with the twelve (male) apostles, on the night before he died. Therefore it should be interpreted as a Passover (paschal) meal in which Jesus is assuming the primordial role of the sacrificial lamb for the salvation of humankind.

If all the other meals were inclusive, and this seems to have been a nonnegotiable for Jesus, then the Last Supper consisted of more than just the twelve apostles. Moreover, we know that most, if not all, of the twelve had fled in fear by the time of Jesus' death; if the meal happened sometime close to his imminent death, then some of those scared apostles would have already fled. To suggest that all of them were present at the Last Supper seems to be defying common sense itself.

The specific focus on the Last Supper has been used by the Christian churches for some quite disturbing disempowering outcomes. To the fore is the claim that since it was only males who were at the Last Supper, then only male priests can facilitate the celebration of Eucharist. This seems like a literalist appropriation of Sacred Scripture that desecrates the sacredness of scripture itself, turning one of the most empowering Gospel prerogatives (the commensality) into an ideology, validating power and privilege for a clerical elite.

The sacrificial element also needs serious review. Linking Eucharist primarily, if not exclusively, to the Passover ritual of the sacrificial lamb suggests elements contrary to the spirit of the Companionship of Empowerment. It has birthed a dangerously misguided spirituality in which pain and suffering are valued in their own right as perquisites for salvation from sin and the reassurance of redemption hereafter.

The emphasis on sacrifice also enhances a patriarchal bias scrutinized at length by Nancy Jay (1992), with deleterious consequences for women over many centuries. "Sacrificial traditions," she writes, "have rarely been questioned about the ways they are grounded in the social relations of reproduction or about the ways they work to achieve male domination" (Jay 1992, 147).

Contextualizing the Last Supper as a sacrificial ritual disempowers both humans and God's creation, generating passivity and subservience and an eventual resolution of escape to a world hereafter. It also undermines what seems to have been the foundational significance of the libation (the cup), widely understood today in the vein of atonement theory: "so that sins may be forgiven" (words added only in the Gospel of Matthew: 26:28), when in fact the original intent was allegedly a political counter to imperial power and a forthright denunciation of it, invoking instead the hope for more empowering ways of being in the world.

## Cosmic Commensality

The feeding of the five thousand (Mark 6:34–44; Matt. 14:13–21; Luke 9:10–17; John 6:1–13) is a legend that puzzles and enthralls even non-Christians. Is it just a spiritual, symbolic para-ble, or is something more mysterious transpiring? The popular exegete William Barclay has proposed an ingenious resolution to the puzzle. He suggests that in Jesus' day people tended to take food with them when they traveled, and selfishly guarded what food they had in case of emergency. Barclay suggests that many, if not all, the people in the crowd of five thousand probably have food, but they all are guarding what they possess. Jesus sees a young boy — symbol of childlike trust — with a lunch; he asks the boy to share some of his food with himself! People watch in amazement, and progressively begin to do the same for each other till everybody is fed and nourished. There is no divine multipli-cation, but there is human sharing and empowerment of a truly miraculous nature.

In one rendering of this story, we see the disciples fretful and fearful for their comfort and perhaps for their safety. Trying to procure food for people feels like such a burden. Or is it a case that they are petrified by the prospect that they themselves might have to endure such hunger at some stage? Jesus refuses to enter-tain any of their doubts or reservations and insists that food must be procured. There is no place for food shortages in the dispen-sation of the open table. God's unconditional generosity must never be compromised, a challenge that lends itself readily to the creative mind of the poet:

## Who Fed the Five Thousand and with What?

*They were weary and lonely, the disciples themselves,*
*Having buried the Baptist now martyred.*
*And they hungered for food to maintain their strength,*
*Re-establish the course they had chartered.*
*And the people who pestered began to annoy*
*Towards the end of a day feeling burdened.*
*And they pleaded with Jesus to send them away*
*And provide for themselves mid their kindred.*

*And then comes the retort they did not expect,*
*'twas their duty the hungry to nourish.*
*"But where can we find food for this massive gang*
*In a place where there's no food to flourish?"*
*But Jesus discerned the twinkling eye*
*Of a boy with a sandwich worth sharing.*
*And how many more had provisions as well*
*Mid the fear and the risk of declaring!*

*The disciples so hungry were aching inside,*
*But first they must tender their service.*
*Arrange them in groups, then seated at ease*
*And bring forth the food from their purses.*
*And Jesus declares the blessing so rare*
*When the generous Spirit sustains us.*
*And the little boy's sandwich remains to this day*
*A symbol so powerful and gracious.*

*This miracle story all Gospels proclaim,*
*How a crowd could be fed with such caring.*
*We thought 'twas a magic of multiplying lots*
*But in truth, 'twas miraculous sharing.*
*Creation abundant — there's plenty for all,*
*Every time that we celebrate eucharist.*
*Transcending the fear which traps us in greed,*
*A nourishing Sabbath our future.*

*Alas, the disciples remained rather dumb,*
*And argued 'bout bread to sustain them.*
*While the people so grateful, their baskets were filled*
*With the crumbs from the meal that maintained them.*
*Let's never forget the mandate so clear:*
*To feed everyone at our table.*
*No more deprivation, starvation, or pain,*
*Seek justice as much as we're able!*

Jesus shared food with a wide range of people at the table of radical inclusiveness, marking not merely a revolutionary concept with far-reaching implications for the indigenous culture of his day, but also carrying cosmic potentialities that have gone largely unobserved. It has been suggested that for Jesus the open table is an icon of both local and cosmic empowerment. It represents a dispensation of communal sharing in which nobody need ever be hungry. By the same token, it denotes the cosmic creation that nourishes all God's people abundantly, and, that being the case, all forms of charitable almsgiving subvert the cosmic abundance that God intends for every earthly creature.

Here we embrace one of the most neglected dimensions of Gospel empowerment. The economic system adopted by all modern governments declares that *scarcity* is the principle value we encounter in the whole of creation. With the publication of Adam Smith's *The Wealth of Nations* in 1776, the science of modern economics was born. *Scarcity* became the new economic principle and remains so to the present day. In an influential 1932 essay, Lionel Robbins defined economics as the science which studies human behavior as a relationship between ends and *scarce* means which have alternative uses. The concept of *scarcity* became a foundational element in our understanding of economics. As Marion Grau (2004) illustrates so skillfully, modern *homo economicus* is a variant of the hysterical male who believes scarcity of goods and scarcity of salvation belong to the same bankrupt way of viewing reality.

A resource is considered scarce when its availability is not enough to meet its demand. Scarcity is based on the idea that oftentimes a limited supply of goods or services comes up against an ever increasing demand for it and that, as such, every effort must be made to ensure its proper utilization and distribution so as to avoid inefficiency. Most goods and services can be defined as scarce since individuals desire more of them than they already possess (scarcity is maintained by demand). Those that are readily abundant are referred to as free goods. This economic philosophy, with scarcity as a central focus, must be one of the best-kept secrets of all time: pragmatically attractive but spiritually disastrous.

The principle of *scarcity* became the rationale and justification for fierce competition, an open playing field in which the "invisible hand" of the market will assure the best and most productive outcome. Here the market is assigned *semi-divine status.* The political divine right has now seeped from politics into economics. Today, they still function, hand-in-glove. And the consequent brutality of the system, leaving most of humanity disempowered for most of the time, and the earth's resources usurped, exploited, and consumed to the advantage of the rich and powerful, is postulated as a necessary outcome for an efficient economic system. Efficient for those consumed by self-interest, but certainly not congenial to adult wisdom, nor can it be considered to be spiritually or ethically sustainable in any serious sense.

The icon of the open table is grossly misconstrued in order to justify a flawed economic theory. The basic principle of God's creation — and of Gospel commensality — is *abundance,* not scarcity. There are abundant resources on earth to sustain and nourish the entire web of life — including the feeding of the human population — provided the resources are accessed and used in an equitable, just, and sustainable fashion. Instead of neo-classical economics we need what Sallie McFague (2000, 100ff.) calls *ecological economics:*

> The big picture is lost; it is as if the human economy takes place in a vacuum, in isolation from any setting, any limits, any laws other than its own. Hence, the difference of "who we are" in these two economic paradigms is striking: the one (neo-classical) begins with individual human beings and their desire for material goods, while the other (ecological) with human beings as a species, a very needy one, dependent

on a complex but vulnerable living space. The first view says we are consumers of nature's wealth; the other view, that we are members of nature's household.

For the early Christians, the empowerment activated through the practice of commensality regenerated a whole new sense of what it means to belong to the household. It entails an all-embracing inclusiveness, devoid of class distinctions, ethnicity, purity regulations, or social status. But it also embraces a cosmic, planetary worldview that cries out for global justice, so that all can avail themselves of the abundance with which God endows the creative universe. In truth, John Dominic Crossan could describe this new empowering vision as a terror to the powers of the day, when he wrote: "Generous almsgiving may be conscience's last refuge against the terror of open commensality" (Crossan 1991, 341).

## Inner Empowerment

In the light of the above reflections we can now revisit the text of Luke 17:21, usually rendered "The Kingdom of God is within you." As indicated in chapter 2, many scholars favor "among you" or "in your midst." Inspired by the research of the Italian scripture scholar Ilaria Ramelli (2009), who persuasively argues for the priority of "within you," I want to uncover some insights that enhance empowerment from within, and link at another level with the empowering potential of the open table. The "within-ness" of God's New Reign evokes a call to be centered on that which really matters by developing the contemplative gaze to see the empowering sacredness of everything in God's creation. It inculcates the wisdom to judge wisely and act proactively for the empowerment of all. With the two or three gathered in God's name, it empowers us to see the divine in our midst as the internal truth that generates all possibilities.

Let's imagine what it must have been like for those disenfranchised people to be gathered around a meal with Jesus or
to have been the beneficiaries of the miraculous sharing in the
large crowds. They felt accepted, embraced, loved, not harshly
judged anymore, but also, I suspect, challenged to collaborate
in empowering justice for the common good. They would have
felt better within themselves — a kind of psychological affirmation — but in all probability they would have grown in their
appreciation and understanding of the goodness of everything
surrounding them in the cosmic web of life. And Jesus, being
the Immanuel in their midst, would move their attention away
from a God-image of an external judging patriarch to that of a
mutually empowering friend (cf. John 15:15: "I no longer call
you servants, *but friends*"), radically immersed in the human and
planetary sphere. Yes indeed they would come to see and understand that the Companionship of Empowerment (the Kingdom)
belongs to the realm of the "within" precisely because it feels so
real, right there in their midst.

And yet they are not left with a mere human construct, confirm-
ing their human comfort zones. Things have changed — indeed, to
a degree in which they will never again see life in the same way.
Some commentators read this transformation in more mystical
terms, drawing liberally on the Gospel of Thomas and suggesting
Gnostic foundations for faith in Jesus. Cynthia Bourgeault intro-
duces her book *The Wisdom Jesus* (2008) with this passage from
the Gospel of Thomas (2):

> If you are searching you must not stop until you find. When
> you find, however, you will become troubled. Your confu-
> sion will give way to wonder. In wonder you will reign over
> all things. Your sovereignty will be your rest.

The wisdom from within is essentially about seeking and
searching and never resting ideologically in any one creed or
doctrine. Discipleship in the Companionship of Empowerment

involves a transformation of consciousness (Bourgeault 2008, 24), always called to be open to deeper wisdom at the service of larger life, in the heart of God's creation. The inner depths and the outer breadth come from the same inspiring source, the Holy Spirit of God. And it becomes incarnate in the historical Jesus in a more explicit archetypal way, a guiding and challenging model for us all to emulate, so that we too can become other Christs for each other and for our world.

## Take and Eat

Taken at its face value, the discourse on the Bread of Life in John's Gospel (John 6:25–59) sounds dangerously close to cannibalism. Scholars and commentators will point out, of course, that nothing in John's Gospel, and least of all the discourse on the Bread of Life, should be taken literally. Symbolic interpretation must always take priority. Throughout John's Gospel the writer seems to be depicting Jesus as the new Moses (see Day 1998), and just as the former Moses fed the hungering people in the desert (with manna from heaven) so the new Moses nourishes in a more emphatic way by giving of his own self as food for hungering hearts.

Commensality, however, denotes a great deal more than counteracting human hunger, whether understood materially or spiritually, a dualistic distinction that makes no sense in terms of the empowerment envisaged in the new Companionship. It is the prophetic contestation of power itself that poses the greatest challenge. Those called to participate in the open table must never again close or terminate any open, empowering space. No hierarchy, magisterium, structure, or ritual must be allowed to hinder the inclusive, empowering hospitality that the open table denotes.

Already in the first century, the Christian church began to betray this empowering ideal. In Matthew 22:11–14, we read of the guest master expelling a guest from the wedding feast to which all had been invited unconditionally. Within a few decades the celebration of Christian Eucharist became anchored in a plethora of rites and rubrics, eventually evolving into a theology that has become dangerously ideological in our time. The dangerous memory of the open table has been heavily domesticated and its nourishing empowerment has been seriously curtailed.

The foundational theology itself needs to be realigned with the spirituality of commensality. Isolating one Gospel story, namely, the Last Supper, as the springboard for our Eucharistic theology — thus bypassing the other stories of food-sharing — is a tragic example of manipulation and distortion. Using that same narrative to claim priority for a male priesthood is even a greater desecration. Much of the rhetoric on the Eucharist as sacrifice is based on a reappropriation of the tradition of the Paschal Lamb in the Hebrew scriptures, thus forging links with an atonement theology that is extensively critiqued in our time. A more fertile line of enquiry might be that of the funerary meals, created by the women to commemorate and celebrate the departed one(s), as Kathleen Corley (2010) graphically illustrates.

The popular perception that Eucharistic change — whether understood as transubstantiation or transignification — is activated by a priest uttering special words under a divine mandate grossly misrepresents what Eucharist is about and seriously undermines its empowering grace. It also undermines the foundational meaning of the Eucharist as a sacred meal ritually celebrating God's desire to nourish throughout every aspect of creation. Christians tend to consider the bread and the cup as representing the food and drink of the Eucharist, but in fact, the bread represents the entire meal in terms of the reception of nourishing food. The ritual of the cup represents what would have happened *after* the meal proper: the *libation*, which in the Greek and Roman banquets was a tribute to a god or to the emperor and in early Christian times took on a prophetic subversive significance as a tribute to Jesus as the primary source of empowerment for the Christian people.

The early church may have foreseen these deviations and to circumvent them developed a more empowering sense of Eucharistic spirituality. It placed the primary focus not on the Last Supper (e.g., not mentioned in the Didache) or on priesthood, and less so on pronouncing words that would change the bread and wine, but rather on the invocation of the Holy Spirit as the heart and soul of Eucharistic ritual (see Crockett 1989). The invocation of the Holy Spirit (Latin: *epiclesis*) upon the people and upon the elements of bread and wine remains to this day a central element of Eucharistic theology — taught in most seminaries, but forgotten in most Eucharistic liturgies.

By reclaiming this central role for the Holy Spirit in the celebration of the Eucharist, the early church was inadvertently endorsing the Companionship of Empowerment, which itself is birthed and energized by the Holy Spirit of God as is everything in God's creation. And with this realignment, we stand a much better chance of honoring the prophetic dynamism of the open table.

If Eucharist is to be an empowering ritual aligned to the inspiring model of the open table, then the invocation of the Holy Spirit needs to become a prerogative of the worshiping community with the priest acting as facilitator of the ritual. Nothing outrageous in that suggestion as the church has always taught that the role of the priest (and the bishop) is to be the *servus servorum Dei* (servant of the servants of God), modeled elegantly by the mother in her conventional role in the Jewish Shabbat meal, the first model adopted by the early church in its celebration of Eucharist.

Ways of celebrating Eucharist that fail to honor the empowering potential of Gospel commensality will leave the people of God hungering for true food. It will also fail to conscientize people with regard to the serious economic and political colonization of food, leading to mass starvation and exploitation in our world.

Every Eucharist is a political statement and an economic challenge. Liturgies that fail to embrace such global outreach will also fail to touch the deep places in the human heart that can be satisfied only by the liberating and empowering bread of life.

On that note, I'd like to end this chapter with an oft-cited inspiring quotation from Raimundo Panikkar:

> The great challenge today is to convert the sacred bread into real bread, the liturgical peace into political peace, the worship of the Creator into reverence for the Creation, the Christian praying community into an authentic human fellowship. It is risky to celebrate the Eucharist. We may have to leave it unfinished, having gone first to give back to the poor what belongs to them.

## Chapter Seven

# Decoding Gender Marginalization

*It is not just that the church fails to see the full complexities of being human, but that it fails to see the full complexity of Christ.* — GERARD LOUGHLIN

*If we are taking incarnation seriously, we cannot worry about decency; we have to embrace diversity in all its challenging forms.* — LISA ISHERWOOD

Sexism, and particularly heterosexism, was a central feature of the male domination system that prevailed in early Christian times. It created disempowerment on a massive scale, but it was so subsumed into the mainstream culture that most people never thought of challenging it, and those who did were quickly and efficiently marginalized.

Marginalization and victimization are the inevitable consequences of patriarchal dominance and control. Men are perceived to be strong, so women must be weak. Recall one of several damning statements of Aristotle: "A woman is to say a sterile man... a woman, so to say, is a mutilated man; menstruations are sperm, but an impure sperm" (quoted by Alaine Rouselle 1989, 45). The male procreates in the power of the seed; the woman is the passive material for the fertilization of the life-giving seed (a theory that has been totally disproved in modern science). Woman is that fickle, hysterical half of humanity, Aristotle's and Aquinas's misbegotten male. Serious stuff must not be entrusted to them. Men alone are endowed with true rationality.[9]

111

On closer examination we note that nobody wins in this system. Although the negative impact on women is more obvious, most men also suffer deprivation and degradation under this regime. Most men don't measure up to the fullness of manhood, an outcome felt painfully by many males today with internationally depleted levels of libido and fertility.

So too in the Christian Gospels. We see both women and men who have been disempowered. Ivone Gebara (2002, 7, 118) helps us to confront this harsh truth when she writes:

> We need only to remember that in Christianity the aspect of sacrifice that is salvific is basically male. Male sacrifice is the only kind that redeems and restores life; male blood is the only blood of any value.... To cling to the Cross of Jesus as the major symbol of Christianity ultimately affirms the path of suffering and male martyrdom as the only way to salvation and to highlight injustice towards women and humanity. All the suffering of women over the centuries of history would be deemed useless by such a theology of history.

In the case of Gospel women the disempowerment is much more pernicious, often accompanied by a blatant sense of inferiority and even invisibility. However, many of the male characters, including the so-called twelve apostles, are also disempowered and victimized. Conditions resulting in bodily dysfunction — deaf, blind, crippled — seem to be rooted in internalized oppression, already noted in chapter 5 above. In the story of the man lowered through the roof (Mark 2:1–12), the primary focus is not on restoring his ability to walk properly, but on the forgiveness of sin. The burden of guilt seems to be the cause of his paralysis.

## Outstanding Marys

For many rank-and-file Christians, Mary the mother of Jesus takes a place of honor in their faith and devotion. In Western

Marian spirituality, Mary tends to be depicted as a humble, obe-dient servant, in the guise of a white Western female, head bowed, eyes downcast, hands joined, the proverbial bride of Christ, par-odied as the model of divine abandonment. Deprived of all that belongs uniquely to women as fertile sexual birthers (the arche-typal meaning of *virginity*), her womanhood is objectified as a classical Aristotelian passive, biological organism (see Isherwood and McPhillips 2008, 117ff.). As if the Christian church had real-ized its cruel defeminization, it tries to rectify the imbalance by a special intervention of the Holy Spirit. Not surprisingly, the dehumanized bride of Christ has been extensively used through-out Christendom to subjugate and ostracize women, often to the point of total invisibility.

What a different sense of Mary we get upon reading the empowering narrative provided by Elizabeth Johnson (2002). As a typical Palestinian woman, even when we retain her role as mother and homemaker, cultural analysis suggests that in order simply to survive Mary would have been a robust, cre-ative, innovative person, upholding hope against great odds, in the impoverished and politically inferior conditions of the time. In her cultural context she would be a woman of dark skin, whom later history strove to honor in depictions of the Black Madonna.

Next we come to another Mary of the Gospels, one whose Gospel rehabilitation has made significant strides in recent times, although few in formal church circles acknowledge this fact: Mary Magdalene, already named by St. Augustine as the apostle to the apostles, and described by Jane Schaberg (2004, 79) as "the madwoman in Christianity's attic." In popular Christian lore she is often labeled as a prostitute — a notion that was popularized by Pope St. Gregory the Great — the one from whom Jesus cast out seven demons. According to this portrayal, her primary worth lies in the fact that she became a repentant sinner.

It seems to me that we need a lot of imagination to reclaim the real Mary Magdalene. In this endeavor I am encouraged by Ivone

Gebara (2002, 131), when she writes: "Beyond what is imagined by reason, there is something imagined by desire, poetry, beauty. This concept of the imagination bets on life without mathematical certitude; it bets simply because life is worth being loved and lived to the full."

Let's cross the first hurdle, by adopting the queer reading on Mary Magdalene, explored by Martin Hugo and Cordavo Quero (in Althaus-Reid 2006, 81–110). Let's assume that Mary Magdalene was an actual prostitute! Why does that have to be the subject of so much moral indignation in a culture where prostitution was legal and was a publicly recognized feature of life and culture? Many prostitutes came from noble families; some were quite wealthy, literate, and educated. And to what extent is the allegation being invoked because the male patriarchy of the day can't tolerate the key role Magdalene is playing in the life and ministry of Jesus? A backlash against a *woman prophet* as Schaberg (2004, 80) intimates. Or might it be more a derogatory depiction of the Gospel writers, because they feel they must keep male leadership to the fore in the emerging church, thus sidelining the first witnesses to the Resurrection, and probably the very ones who birthed the church in its nascent years!

And if Mary Magdalene was an "indecent" woman, what difference would that have made to Jesus? He seemed to favor moral outcasts in the Companionship of Empowerment. Why allow the church's long misogynist history and its often cruel denunciation of human sexuality to distract us from the dangerous memory of a Gospel faith that in the language of Gustavo Gutiérrez was not that interested in personal morality, but was strongly focused on the empowerment of nonpersons?

An empowering portrait of Mary Magdalene might also borrow from the novelist Margaret George (2002), who suggests that Mary was a divorced woman, effectively forced from her marriage and home by an extended family who could not accept her radical feminist ideals. Add to that some of the insights from the opening chapter of this book on possible symbolic interpretations of demon possession, one begins to wonder if the seven evil spirits represent the internal trauma — perhaps something akin to a nervous breakdown — that Mary experienced because of the painful ostracization she suffered at the hands of a petrified, patriarchal culture.

Kathleen Corley (2002, 33, 160) considers Mary Magdalene to have been a fisherwoman, which helps to forge the affiliation with the other apostles, as it did for them, the fishing context may have provided the initial integration into discipleship with Jesus. Karen King (2003) supplies one of the better commentaries on the half-missing document now known as the Gospel of Mary, in which Mary is portrayed as a confidante of Jesus, often comprehending the tasks of discipleship with great wisdom and insight to a point that creates jealousy and resentment among the male followers, specifically with Peter. Even if the evidence for such a claim was insurmountable, those who drew up the canon of the scriptures in early Christian centuries would certainly not have embraced such subversive, empowering information.

There are not many allusions to Mary Magdalene in the Gospels, and she is never allowed to speak. She is a liminal character kept on the wings. In Mark's Gospel, she — with the other women — remains silent at the end and leaves the tomb crippled by fear. After all, having portrayed the male disciples in such a negative light, how could Mark bring himself to portray the women more favorably? Christian history would never forgive him for that. Yet despite all the attempts at subversion, the truth for Mary Magdalene seems to be breaking through, with an energy for empowerment that could radically change the future face of Christianity.[10]

## Empowering Women into Visibility

Most scripture scholars today acknowledge that women in the time of Jesus were relegated to passive, inferior roles, often treated as slaves to provide for dominant male needs and expected to do so without seeking recognition or recompense. Joanna Dewey (1997) provides a useful overview, noting that Matthew, Mark, and Luke are filled with female characters who interact with Jesus in a single episode but who do not appear in the story again. Commenting on the portrayal of women in the healing narratives Dewey (1997, 57) writes:

> The stories involving men are on average longer than the ones involving women, and the women are shown speaking less often than the men. The women are less visible in the healing narratives, not only in terms of overall numbers, but also in terms of lesser mimetic development when they do occur. Luke, while including the largest number of stories about women, presents them with the least mimetic emphasis.

Several commentators note on the various roles attributed to women in Gospel lore, including the benevolent and empowering attitude toward women revealed by Jesus (cf. Pagola 2009, 209–30; also, Bauckham 2002; Taylor and Taylor 2004). However, there is an aura of invisibility in many of these accounts that a strategy of empowerment for our time can no longer leave in abeyance. A few statistics illuminate the critical issue.

In the Old Testament, of the 1,426 people given names, only 111 of them are female. In the four canonical Gospels, 15 women are named, 3 being from the Old Testament, cited in Matthew's genealogy. Eight women are named as disciples: Joanna, Martha and Mary of Bethany, Mary Magdalene, Mary the mother of James and Joses, Mary the wife of Cleopas, Salome, and Susannah. In the Gospel of Luke, which some commentators regard as more women-friendly, 39 men are named but only 10 women. In the teaching of Jesus in Luke, women are mentioned 18 times contrasted to the 158 times in which men occur.

Throughout the Gospels as in the allied literature from the Roman and Greek worlds of the day, women tend to be described in terms of men, as spouse, parent, or offspring. We have stories about Peter's mother-in-law, the daughter of Jairus, the Syrophoenician woman, the Samaritan woman, and in all cases the women have no names. The two people on the Emmaus road are assumed to be husband and wife; he is named (Cleopas), she remains unnamed.

Despite the fact that women in the Gospels seem to be relegated to inferior roles and cast within the prevailing patriarchal culture of submission and invisibility, most scholars go on to argue that Jesus adopted a very different stance, treating women with dignity and respect, including them in table fellowship, endorsing their participation in the Companionship of Empowerment. On a few occasions — the woman anointing his feet (Luke 7:36–50) and the Samaritan woman (John 4:4–42) — Jesus clearly transgresses the patriarchal and cultural expectations, with a damning verdict of the misogynist culture.

The story of the Samaritan woman has been subjected to a range of questionable interpretations, particularly in popular spiritual literature, where she tends to be viewed as the immoral woman now converted to true discipleship. If we honor the primacy of a symbolic interpretation — which scholars have long suggested for the whole of John's Gospel — then we more readily see the allusion to the woman's five husbands as a reference to five successive corrupt rulers in the land of Samaria. In which case, the woman is engaging Jesus in a highly symbolic theological conversation, and it really takes poetry to draw forth the incredible empowerment evoked in this narrative:

## The Samaritan Woman

*The Samaritan woman they greet me,*
*Please call me Photini by name.*
*And I relish my place at the wellsprings*

*Contributing to Jacob's fame.*
*This country of mine is Samaria,*
*Long hated in biblical lore.*
*But our parable fame is impressive,*
*The truth we convey is decisive,*
*And the wisdom we hold is excessive*
*For the hearts that discern the truth.*
*So probe the recesses of Wisdom*
*And literalize not the facts.*
*'Cause the Gospel of John is symbolic;*
*Often truth is revealed in the cracks.*

*We broke all the laws of the scripture*
*By sharing a vessel to drink*
*And a rabbi alone with a woman*
*Was another infringement to link.*
*Transgressing our ethnic distinctions*
*We chose to build bridges anew.*
*While birthing a wisdom transgressive,*
*Our dialogue was deep and impressive,*
*And we theologized quite excessive*
*Which the Gospel of John fails to note.*
*It clings to the male at the forefront*
*With me in a secondary role,*
*But in fact it was I did the pacing*
*Empowering a dialogue so whole.*

*I welcomed his bold invitation*
*To outgrow the worship we knew*
*Transcending the mountain and city*
*In the power of the Spirit's fresh hue.*
*My five metaphorical husbands*
*The Gospel of John misconstrues.*
*Five rulers immersed in corruption,*
*My country in sacred disruption,*

*Crying out for true liberty's option*
*A marriage bond yet to be sealed.*
*It had nothing to do with my personal fate*
*As moralists like to impute.*
*Our dialogue was cued to a symbolic depth,*
*Towards the dream of another repute.*

*A people so battered and shattered in fate*
*Found it hard to accept my new vision.*
*They would rather I drew the water in haste*
*And abide by my servile condition.*
*But I knew I'd encountered a wisdom so rare*
*The freedom and hope we had dreamed for.*
*They flocked to the source of freedom to see,*
*They checked for themselves the truth of my plea,*
*And they basked in the promise of a new liberty*
*With a strangely misogynist twist!*
*For the Gospel of John distorts to negate*
*What I as a woman had birthed.*
*"We have heard him ourselves, get out of the way,*
*We'll trust only what we've contested."*
*Despite the rejection and the hurt set aflame,*
*Despite the description, ignoring my name,*
*Some day we might rewrite what's been misconstrued*
*Round the well of true wisdom where truth can't be fooled.*

When it comes to the treatment of women in the Gospels, often Jesus seems to be playing an ambivalent — even a contradictory — role. A few scholars support the analysis of Kathleen Corley (2002), who exposes some serious flaws and limitations on how Jesus treats women. Even if we attribute these deviations to the Gospel writers (rather than to Jesus) we are still left with the personal and pastoral dilemma of sacred texts that are in conflict with the radical inclusiveness and empowerment of the new reign of God. Some examples can be explained as human error —

which I don't find to be incompatible with an empowering sense of incarnation (see chapter 9 below) and others can be viewed anew with the insights of postcolonial studies. However, we are still left with a dilemma for which there is not an easy resolution.

Meanwhile, there is widespread agreement that both Jesus and Paul included women among their disciples. Much more controversial, but with growing evidence to support it, is the claim that some of those women played roles far more crucial than some of the twelve apostles. We have already encountered Mary Magdalene, whose role as apostle to the apostles seems to be gaining acceptance and approval among a growing body of contemporary scholars. If this claim is eventually substantiated then indeed the Companionship of Empowerment will become a dangerous memory of enormous import.

Scholars have also been reclaiming the significant role of female discipleship in the ministry of St. Paul. It appears that in the early stages of his ministry, a great deal was jointly shared with the woman Thecla (Crossan and Reed 2004, xii–xiv, 120–23). Borg and Crossan (2009, 51–52) indicate that in Romans 16:1–16, of the twenty-seven Christian leaders cited, ten are women and seventeen are men, but of those singled out for special attention, five are women and six are men. In Galatians 4:11 and 1 Corinthians 15:10, Paul, describing his dedicated apostolic activity, uses for himself the verb *kopiao:* meaning "to work hard." In Romans 16:6, 12, he uses the same verb four times, applying it to a woman in each case.

Perhaps most significant of all in the Pauline corpus is the character Phoebe, who is entrusted with carrying to Rome the letter to the Romans (16:1–2). This is no mere equivalent to a modern postal service. She would have to read the letter (possibly in auspicious gatherings), preach on it, and explain details to her various audiences. In Gospel language, she would empower them in the power of the Word. Obviously, illiteracy and lack of formal education did not adversely affect women as widely as we have been led to believe.

Against this background of mixed fortunes characterized by ambiguity and ambivalence, how do *we* reclaim Gospel wisdom so that women are truly included in our future commitment to the Companionship of Empowerment? This is a hermeneutical challenge for all involved in the work of interpretation and poses a more formidable challenge for our use of scripture in liturgy and worship. We easily dispense with texts that are clearly in conflict with liberating values in our time, e.g., "slaves obey your masters" (Eph. 6:5; Col. 3:22) or "wives submit to your husbands" (Eph. 5:22; Col. 3:18–19). Just ignoring such texts is a safe but rather immature way to deal with the dilemma. Might it not be a more adult and empowering response to consciously remove such texts, or rewrite them in a way that honors the alternative wisdom of our time?

As an interim measure, I propose that we revisit such texts with the guiding light of poetry rather than prose. Poetry evokes an alternative consciousness; it plumbs the depths with another kind of wisdom, more fluid, playful, and imaginative. As I illustrate throughout this book and in a previous work (O'Murchu 2009), poetry can be particularly empowering to delineate an enlarged and enfleshed portrait of those condemned to invisibility in Gospel prose.

## Male Disempowerment

In Greek ethics, friendship is deemed possible only between men of independent means. Women, slaves, and servants are excluded, but also men who do not measure up to the autonomy and self-sufficiency defined as necessary for real men. With Hellenistic influences encroaching on the culture of Jesus, with patriarchal bias already in evidence in the Hebrew background, and many men oppressed or marginalized because of the burden of Roman taxation, it is possible, and even probable, that the prevailing oppression undermined men as well as women. In fact, the Gospels cite examples of men who were significantly disempowered.

The emphasis on male disempowerment can be more subtle and complex. Possession by evil spirits seems to be a particularly debilitating condition as well as being socially ostracizing. Interestingly, such demonic influence does not seem to be linked with ritual impurity; possessed people are feared, but not seen as spiritual outcasts. The psychological context may be highly significant but difficult to discern two thousand years later. Several encounters narrated in the Gospels portray the possessed person as articulating unmet needs, crying out in desperation, addressing Jesus in divine titles used by Roman emperors.

One of the most graphic examples of male demonic marginalization is that of the Gerasene demoniac (Mark 5) already explored in chapter 5 above. His plight makes a graphically disturbing read when echoed in poetry (O'Murchu 2009, 71–73). In a culture where male identity was strongly focused on being the breadwinner and the primary provider and protector of the family institution, not to be able to fulfill that role would in itself catapult many males into deep depression, hopelessness, and insanity.

The somatic impact of such degradation is almost certainly at the root of the examples in the Gospels of people — most of the recorded examples are males — debilitated through blindness, deafness, or the inability to speak. Poetic insight helps to break open the inner darkness of being trapped and made to feel so helpless, as illustrated in the story of the deaf mute (Mark 7:31–37):

## Opening the Closet of Enforced Silence

*I could not speak correctly, 'cause I could not hear a word*
*An affliction I inherited from youth.*
*But worse than my affliction,*
*Was the pain of interdiction,*
*Like a victim of eviction,*

*Allegedly impure.*
*I was labeled an outsider*
*Unworthy a provider,*
*In a culture that so brutally condemned the struggling poor.*

*I could not speak correctly, so they never asked my name,*
*And anonymous the Gospels leave me too.*
*I'm ritually infested,*
*By my family rejected,*
*And my spirits are dejected,*
*Like a social renegade.*
*My hearing retardation,*
*And stuttering frustration,*
*And just as hope was running out, empowering grace broke*
*    through.*

*I had heard of many healers — who had little time for me*
*Till the Nazarene invited me by name.*
*A ritual for invoking,*
*A gentle touch for stroking,*
*Eph'phatha for an opening,*
*That broke loose my inner bind.*
*What a burden he had lifted,*
*What a hope he gently shifted,*
*Empowering me and others to be healers for our kind.*

*And there's no more anonymity*
*For the one who's deaf and mute.*
*By name they call me Benjamin,*
*And I proudly claim my truth!*

Another vivid example is of the man waiting for thirty-eight
years before anybody would even help him to get to the pool.
At the time of Jesus, forty was considered ripe old age. The only
other time the phrase thirty-eight years appears in the Bible is
in Deuteronomy 2:14 describing the length of time the Jews had

spent in the wilderness, where they received the five books of the Law (represented in the five porticoes). In keeping with the rich use of symbolism in John's Gospel (5:1–18), the cripple by the pool in his painful predicament probably represents Israel in its felt deprivation — and its longing for God's liberation.

Indeed, the suggestive possibilities may stretch to the point of questioning the entire inheritance of patriarchal religion, with its crippling effects even on the very ones who worked so diligently to safeguard and promote it, namely, the men. Poetry itself can become a dangerous memory; such are the depths to which it leads our reflections:

## Paralyzed in the Burden of Time

*Thirty-eight long years*
*Abandoned and deserted in an alien place,*
*Oblivious to the five pillars*
*Of law and covenant of a sacred race.*
*The people of Israel wandered,*
*And in vain they wondered,*
*Like the lame, blind, and paralyzed!*
*Would anyone ever come and lead them*
*To the energetic waters, the wellspring of new hope?*

*Thirty-eight long years,*
*So despondent, he did not even ask.*
*Perhaps, he saw no point,*
*Mid petrified fear, one does not risk.*
*But messianic hope breaks through*
*And it does not take too many words*
*To raise the shattered spirit,*
*As the healing waters rise within!*
*The pool is now redundant, as the Spirit overflows.*

*Take up that mat and walk,*
*Come home from exile too long known.*

*And engage the powers of darkness,*
*Camouflaged in leaders of renown.*
*Demented by Sabbath law and legal tract,*
*Blind and deaf to all who journey home.*
*Our refugees, displaced and brutalized by far,*
*Sheltering in anguish beneath the porticoes,*
*Waiting for the wellspring, a glimmer of small hope.*

*Why do we abandon hope? Why condemn*
*The other to the abyss of despair?*
*Those who wander lonely roads,*
*The mat, the rucksack, their meager lot.*
*No messianic guru now, other than you and me.*
*We are supposed to be the body of the living Christ!*
*God of Mercy, what a mess we've made,*
*Preoccupied with trivialities so trite*
*While millions ache and hunger for the Spirit of new life.*

The church has long regarded the twelve apostles as the stalwarts of faith in God and in Jesus, but even a cursory reading of the Gospels highlights their fragility and vulnerability. They seem somewhat stuck in the notion that Jesus should be some kind of imperial divine rescuer, and when he fails to live up to their expectations they become quite petrified: Peter, forever needing reassurance to protect his power, and the brothers James and John preoccupied with their own privileged status in the life to come. And when it came to the final crunch, with Judas capitulating to total despair, the rest seem to flee, lest they too might suffer a similar plight.

The malehood they exemplify is at best ambiguous, lacking many of the qualities which men of the time were expected to exhibit. In the vein of a prophetic critique we may wonder if the Gospel texts are trying to highlight the failures of patriarchal manhood rather than its virtues. Whether because of postcolonial collusion or for some other reasons difficult to access, male empowerment in the Gospels seems to know only one basic model, that of patriarchal top-down control. Many of the Gospel male personalities, however, fail dismally in achieving that ideal. Throughout the Gospels, the cult of domination does not appear to be very creative or empowering — for men or for women — and two thousand years later it remains even more problematic.

## What Kind of Male Was Jesus?

Feminist scholars often ask: how can a male embodiment of God be salvific or liberating for women, particularly within the context of a monotheistic religion like Judaism or Christianity? There are also millions of men for whom a male God-figure, invested with kingly power and glory, is anything but empowering. On the contrary, such an imposing figurehead can feel oppressively daunting, leaving even men with feelings of inferiority and unworthiness. The Christian Jesus, with all the trappings of patriarchy and colonialism, is far from being an inspiring and empowering model for either women or men.

And the maleness of Jesus as we glean it from the written and oral sources also seems to be heavily suppressed. The historical Jesus seems to have stood out as being different, unusual, quite odd. His unmarried status would have been a real puzzle for many in his day.[11] His tendency to relate closely with women was unusual, yet he often succumbs to patriarchal genderizing as Kathleen Corley (2002) illustrates. His camaraderie with prostitutes, tax collectors, and other outcasts ruffled many of the normative expectations in his time.

A few scholars have tried to make a case for Jesus being gay, surrounded as he seems to have been by so many males (Goss 1994; 2007; Jennings 2009). It seems to me that the evidence is virtually nonexistent, but the suggestion creates an opening for a far deeper discernment into aspects of his manhood that surface when we search for archetypal clues. If Jesus manifests shamanic characteristics — as well as a prophetic dynamism transgressing conventional boundaries — then, as Halvor Moxnes (2004) illustrates so vividly, his psychosexual identity is likely to be transgressive, queer (as in queer theory), defiant in terms of what was culturally normative. However, in honoring the primacy of the Companionship of Empowerment, as I am striving to do through this book, we can attribute significance to an alternative psychosexual identity only if we can view it as empowering and liberating for a larger sense of life and meaning.

I have long been attracted to the idea of Jesus being *androgynous,* an insight that has received only scant scholarly attention. Scholars such as Rita Nakashima Brock, Elisabeth Schüssler Fiorenza, and Elizabeth Johnson all interpret Jesus against the background of the Wisdom literature in the Hebrew scripture, where Holy wisdom (Sophia) is personalized as a female; only Schüssler Fiorenza veers toward some gender bending in describing Jesus as a *wo/man.*

The androgyne is an *archetype* rather than a literal concept, although as I'll illustrate presently, it does translate into distinctive human behaviorial patterns. In social and psychological terms it is, even to this day, considered to be the ultimate deviancy in psychosexual development, an internal confused state whereby a person cannot clearly differentiate between being male and being female. Biologically, there is no ambiguity — very different from trans-sexualism, and the felt need for gender-changing. (Generally speaking, androgynes do not desire a sex change.)

The androgynous orientation is based on internal psychic dispositions, whereby a person veers naturally toward behaviors stereotypically those of the opposite sex. For example, a man may feel a strong urge to be a homemaker and child-nurturer, to such an extent that he experiences serious health problems trying to maintain a stereotypical high-achievement career. Or a woman may feel much more at home in being a business executive, rather than a mother, carer, or homemaker. These are merely indicators that a person may be predominantly an androgyne. The androgynous state cannot be judged by any set of external criteria because it is essentially an inner disposition with unique qualities of creativity, sensitivity, yearning for completeness, mystical attraction, and often a strong sense of not fitting into the prevailing culture.

Why is androgyny so culturally problematic, even reprehensible? A few reasons come readily to mind:

(a) It forthrightly confronts the dualistic divisions deemed so essential for the effective management of reality. Bisexual people often experience this same antagonism. It is okay to be straight or gay, but bisexuality is deemed to be weird, confused, and confusing because it scrambles the neat binary divisions in which society invests so much meaning and significance.

(b) It threatens prevailing paradigms of an ideal male, and at a time when male identity is already under severe strain, the androgynous archetype is simply too much to take on. Instead we seek to ridicule and subvert the very notion.

(c) For women, historical baggage seems to be a primary block. For much of patriarchal history (some ten thousand years), and frequently in Christian times, a woman could attain a more exalted state by becoming more like a man. We detect echoes of this in early Gnosticism; in the Gospel of Thomas (114); and in the notion of the virile woman, which was common in the Middle Ages (cf. Bynum 1991; Newman 1995). Feminists, who feel they have had to fight hard for women's liberation as women, tend to be suspicious of androgyny, fearing it as another fad that could compromise what has taken so long to achieve.

(d) The psychosexual landscape of our time is already highly amorphous, fluid, and undefined. Tolerating and/or inculturating homosexuality and transgendering is more than

enough for many cultures, and those of a more funda-
mentalist persuasion feel we have already gone too far.
Embracing androgyny feels like anarchy let loose.

This is precisely the reason why we need to entertain the notion
of Jesus as androgynous. The Companionship of Empowerment
is indeed anarchy let loose. All the solid, time-honored dictates of
reason, stability, and security are scrambled. Boundaries are being
transgressed and transformed. Truth is being demolished and
redefined. And most dislocating of all, the guardians of orthodoxy
are demoted from imperial thrones. Today, the scholarly world
labels it *postmodernism;* the fundamentalists call it *anarchy.* The
Christian Gospel calls it the *Companionship of Empowerment.*
And it certainly is a most dangerous memory!

## Jesus and the Protean Self

In an earlier work (O'Murchu 2010), I explored the fluid, tran-
sitional nature of human identity in our time. People morph into
a whole range of identities as circumstances demand. Philip and
Mikela Tarlow (2002) claim — contrary to public opinion — that
this is in fact an indigenous disposition of great age. Our neat conventional ways of managing reality and of sequestering a limited
number of fixed identities through which we relate and function
in the world is a relatively recent evolutionary development, and
not necessarily an indicator of greater strength or maturity.

In the interpretation of many parable and miracle stories in
the Gospels, commentators seem to assume that the empowerment taking place leads to greater self-reliance, independence,
and the ability to function as autonomous human beings. This is
very much a projection from the present onto the past. Although
the Aristotelian understanding of the self-reliant, rational individual had entered both the Roman and Jewish worlds by the

time of Jesus, the program of the Companionship of Empowerment evokes a very different understanding of the human person,
one characterized by a strong sense of relationality rather than
individual autonomy (see chapter 3 above). And the relationality
was not confined merely to other humans; it embraced, at least
subliminally, the entire planetary and cosmic webs of life.

This alternative sense of selfhood — with interdependence and
relationality as its core values and a tendency to bypass the conventional labels associated with race, ethnicity, nationality, and
religion — has been variously named in recent decades. Here I
will adopt the label of the "protean self," used by the American
psychiatrist Robert J. Lifton (1999). Supportive and controversial characteristics are outlined by the Jamaican-American
philosopher Jason Hill (2002; 2009) in his appellation of the
"cosmopolitan" person. Jeremy Rifkin (2009, 554ff.) describes
this new emergence as "the dramaturgical frame of mind." None
of these ideas are as original as initially presumed. For most of
our time on earth, indications are that we lived from within a
strong sense of life experienced as a relational matrix, a feature
discernible to this day in indigenous groups around the world.

I cite these modern examples because they help to reconnect us
with the relational sense of the human person embedded in the
Gospel notion of the Companionship of Empowerment. On this
front, Jesus and the program of the Kingdom of God were many
centuries ahead of postmodernism. And if Jesus considered this
new sense of person paradigmatic for others, with good reason
we can assume he lived it out himself.

At this juncture we run into the limitations of language and the
tendency to juxtapose reality in binary pairs as we commonly do
in the West. In a sense, the androgyne is the ultimate statement
of relational propensity; we could even say that the androgyne
is an archetype of the human capacity for relationship. At this
level where male and female distinctiveness becomes blurred and
fuzzy, is it appropriate to describe Jesus as "him," or to use the

pronoun "himself"? In biological terms Jesus may have been a male, but the challenge of engaging with androgynous identity is that our biology does not define us. The androgyne is defined, not by biology, but by a psychic energy directed toward broad and deep interrelating. The sense of personal value and worth is not based on external determining factors (such as biology), but on an internal lure that defies rational explanation.

## Regenderizing the Gospels

Judith Butler is one of the better-known proponents of post-genderized identity, an oft-cited authority for radical feminist thinkers. For Butler, biology seems relatively unimportant as all forms of human identity, including the appellations of male and female, are culturally produced: "There is no gender identity behind expressions of gender; that identity is performatively con-stituted by the very expressions that are said to be its results" (Butler 1990, 25).

At the heart of the Aristotelian view of the human person is an essentializing of biology, particularly for Aristotle's under-standing of maleness and his consequent derisory disregard for womanhood. In many sciences and religions we idolize biology, requiring a reevaluation that is long overdue. However, getting rid of gender identity entirely as Butler and other postmodernists pro-pose seems to be denying an important feature of organic life. As I understand it, an androgynous identity is about the integration of biological differences and not their elimination.

I suspect that personal difference, including biology, is impor-tant for Jesus and for the Companionship of Empowerment. The richness and complementarity of the different sexes is something to cherish and build on rather than destroy and eliminate. The many stories in the Gospels mediating healing and empowerment seem to regard the person as a composite whole comprising a bio-physical, social, emotional, and spiritual being, all of which are held together by the psychic will-to-meaning. Contrary to Butler, the Christian needs to honor all those dimensions, seeking forever to reweave them into the rich and unique tapestry that constitutes each human life.

In the Gospels we certainly need to revision and revamp the problematic use of gendered and genderized distinctions. In many cases, women are treated with a repressed sense of anonymity, often made invisible and without the power of naming. Men, on the other hand, are cast as the powerful, privileged ones, but when males fail to fulfill that culturally imposed role, then the prevailing culture is merciless in relegating them — not merely into anonymity — but into crippling poverty, slavery, and the erosion of self-worth to the point of insanity.

Championing the cause of empowerment, Jesus seems to opt for a radical envisioning of human identity. Patching up the old wineskin no longer seems adequate or appropriate. "Behold I make all things new" (Rev. 21:5) — including the foundations upon which a new sense of humanity can be constructed. Dualisms are declared defunct, commonalities are more important than differences, relationality transcends independence, and the holarchy replaces the hierarchy. Perhaps most controversial of all, the androgyne seems to surface as the primary expression of God's incarnational presence in our midst.

# Chapter Eight

# Suffering at the Service
# of Empowerment

*Redemption means overcoming all forms of patriarchy....*
*Suffering is a factor in the liberation process, not as a means*
*of redemption, but as the risk that one takes when one strug-*
*gles to overcome unjust systems whose beneficiaries resist*
*change. The means of redemption is conversion, opening up*
*to one another, changing systems of distorted relations, cre-*
*ating loving and life-giving communities of people here and*
*now, not getting oneself tortured to death.*

— ROSEMARY RADFORD RUETHER

Cynthia Bourgeault (2008, 21) makes the interesting observation
that Western Christianity has been preoccupied with salvation
and soteriology — to make up for the flaw left because of the
sin of Adam — whereas Eastern Christianity is much more concerned about the wisdom necessary for good living, which she
calls as *sophiology*. The former emphasizes what Jesus did for
us because essentially we are disempowered, helpless creatures,
while the latter underlines mutual empowerment, a quality of
engagement with life that the historical Jesus embraced as a process of human transformation, and inspired by the primordial
example of Jesus, we can also realize it in our own lives.

In the original Aramaic of Jesus' time, there was no word for
*salvation*. In the Aramaic New Testament, two words are used:
one of these is *chai,* meaning "life" or the verb, "to vivify," and

the other is *p'rak,* which comes from a root meaning "to separate" and invokes the image of one being "rescued" by being "separated" from a threat. This latter meaning clearly echoes the atoning nature of Jesus' death and resurrection, portraying Jesus in the traditional role of the great rescuer.

## Salvation as Wholeness

The Anabaptist theologian Tim Grimsrud (*http://peacetheology .net/*) notes that *salvation* in the Old Testament has to do with *wholeness,* which is regained mainly through healing, law, and sacrifice in order to restore a sense of the covenant community. To gain salvation leads to harmony with God, with other human beings, and with the rest of creation. We need salvation when we live with disharmony, when we experience brokenness instead of wholeness.

The Old Testament begins with a portrayal of creation at peace. However, after the beginning, the Bible presupposes disharmony and brokenness and focuses on the struggle for salvation. Salvation results in healed brokenness, restored health, and wholeness. The Bible presents salvation on three levels: (1) salvation as liberation from the powers of brokenness, (2) salvation as restoration of harmony with God, and (3) salvation as restoration of harmonious human relationships. The Old Testament story places priority on salvation in the first sense (liberation).

The concepts of healing, restoration, and liberation surface strongly in the New Testament, particularly in Pauline theology. In all cases, however, there prevails a popular perception that the initiative is with God (and Jesus) and that humans are essentially passive, unworthy recipients of what is being offered. The empowerment is effectively a one-way stream, and this understanding prevails throughout the history of Christendom, sadly becoming more preoccupied with human depravity and an interpretation of the Christ event strongly focused on divine, salvific intervention.

When we invoke the Companionship of Empowerment, quite a different emphasis comes to the fore. Mutuality enters our discernment. Theologically, the initiative is still with God (as is everything in creation), but humans are perceived in a more benign and proactive way. The image of the vineyard, so often cited in the parables, evokes a collaborative endeavor in which salvation (redemption) is not merely about the human soul, but about the entire web of life, empowered through the work of healing, restoration, and liberation. We move beyond the focus indicating a kind of co-dependent relationality with the prerogative largely if not totally in the hands of the divine rescuer.

There is no empowerment in rescuing. The person being rescued is presumed to be helpless and powerless. She or he is at the mercy of the one doing the rescuing. The plight of passivity, the feeling of being useless and pathetic, undermines all sense of self-worth, dignity, integrity, and that healthy internalization of self-empowerment that is at the basis of all growth and genuine development. We are dealing with an arrested sense of anthropology, unworthy of both God and humanity.

The graphic irony of rescuing is depicted in the Karpman triangle (based on transactional analysis) of *victim — rescuer — persecutor.* A person feeling victimized, or deemed to be so, becomes the focus of the rescuer (who may be motivated consciously or subconsciously). The ensuing co-dependent relationship can easily result in victims switching roles and seeking to persecute the very ones who rescued them — in which case the rescuer becomes the new victim. In the ensuing game, all three players end up brutalizing each other. Power is wreaking havoc, and all semblance of empowerment has been suppressed or was never possible in the first place. This brutal game is often played out in the human arena, a favored patriarchal strategy, frequently validated by the religiosity of redemptive violence.

## The Passion Story

Despite the elaborate details in all four Gospels we know virtually nothing about the passion and death of Jesus. We have a narrative based on the faith-convictions of the early followers, who attempted to make sense out of the untimely death of Jesus by extrapolating from the Hebrew scriptures events and sayings that seemed to be pointing to Jesus, that helped make sense out of his death, and were weaved into a melodramatic story that became the passion narratives in Gospel lore.

If we want something akin to a historical backdrop, we are — as Crossan suggests — on more solid ground when we invoke the first Roman War, of 66–70 C.E., in which the temple in Jerusalem was destroyed and thousands of innocent people were killed. Much of the calamity, injustice, and violence associated with the death of Jesus — and vividly portrayed in Mel Gibson's *The Passion of the Christ* — was probably inspired by that historical event, as was a great deal of the apocalyptic material in Mark 13 and elsewhere in the Gospel narratives.

Of particular interest for the present work is the way in which patriarchal kingly power is woven into the passion narrative of the Gospels and holds the reader in its grip. It feels like a story of high drama and is sometimes depicted as such, when in truth the act of crucifixion was a savage, brutal affair, which no responsible person would want to honor or acclaim. The trials of Jesus make the plot more colorful and alluring — six in all — culminating in Pilate's death sentence for a crime of trying to usurp kingly power (the allegation that Jesus claimed to be king of the Jews). The trials, as described, infringe upon principles of Roman jurisprudence and have long been regarded as fictitious or mock trials at best. So why was it so important for the Gospel writers to include and emphasize these trials?

Are we witnessing an enduring fixation with divine kingship, with Jesus as a perceived messianic prophet who had to be of kingly origin, and therefore would have had to have a fair and just trial? A king could not have been killed without some attempt at juridical justice. So the Gospel writers invent a legal travesty with Jesus consistently depicted as the mythic hero, adorned with kingly might in John 18:37. And after the death of the royal One, the Gospel writers have to make sure that there is something akin to a royal burial. The notion that Jesus' body might have been buried hurriedly and "in shame," as frequently happened to subversives during the Roman-Jewish war (66–70 C.E.), is a prospect that must not even be entertained when dealing with somebody of noble, royal status.[12]

Power, and not sanctity (divinity), is what dictates much of the Passion narrative. And the entire story must be made to look and feel heroic. "The central irony in the passion narratives of the Gospel," writes Joel Marcus (2006, 73), "is that Jesus' crucifixion turns out to be his elevation to kingship." Ideally, as in John's Gospel, the condemned hero must be seen not merely to survive, but to triumph. All too easily then the death becomes an end in itself, the ultimate paradoxical triumph of the hero. Emulation of the death will later be perceived to be necessary for those who are called to discipleship. Correspondingly, the archetypal empowerment of the *life* of Jesus fades into the background and for much of the Christian era was viewed mainly as a preparation for the grand finale, which alone could deliver divine salvation.

In an oft-cited text, Crossan interprets the Passion narrative as *prophecy historicized* rather than history remembered. Key texts and insights from the Hebrew scriptures, especially from the Psalms, Isaiah, the Prophets, and the Wisdom literature, were employed, first, to make sense of the violent and untimely death of Jesus and, second, to augment belief in the messianic status attributed to Jesus by the early followers. The end result is a vastly embellished proclamation, much like a historical tribute to a fallen hero. The downfall of the hero became the alluring myth, while the heroic transformation of Jesus' earthly life and ministry was sidelined and subverted.

Kathleen Corley (2010) supplements our understanding of the embellishment from her study of women's involvement in funerary rites at the time of Jesus. The tradition of lamenting the dead is also known in ancient Greek, Roman, and Jewish literature and in all cases tends to be a female prerogative. We encounter such lamentations in the Hebrew Bible, and Christians have tended to use those texts for the Good Friday church ceremonies. This is quite a complex subject, enacted to empower people to grieve and mourn proactively rather than be disempowered by what Walter Brueggemann calls "the numbness of death" (Brueggemann 1978, 46ff; 1986, 33ff.).

Is this where the first story of Jesus' Passion emerges from? A dirge of honor and tribute to a noble hero — as happened in Hellenistic contexts? According to Kathleen Corley (2010, 2): "Women lamented the dead, *composing elaborate narratives* about the life and cause of death of the deceased, prepared and served funerary meals, and made offerings to the dead at tombs" (emphasis mine). And Corley goes on to assert: "The passion narrative had its origins in a grassroots liturgical context dominated by women and ordinary people.... The existence of a popular liturgical tradition concerning Jesus' death could preclude the existence of an original written version of the passion narrative altogether" (128).

In supporting this intriguing thesis, John Dominic Crossan (in Corley 2010, xii) writes:

Focusing on what men were doing led contemporary male scholars — myself included — to miss where the real action was. Was it what the women were doing that got it all going? And since that ancient exclusion has had permanent and present consequences can we at least recognize it and remedy it at last?

The truth behind the melodramatic detail is not difficult to discern. Crucifixion was a form of death reserved, not even for hardened criminals, but for subversives, for those perceived to be a threat to the prevailing power. Jesus was a subversive, mainly because of how he activated empowerment among the masses. Although some scholars argue that Jesus may have been an anti-Roman protagonist (Brandon 1967), inciting violent rebellion against the Empire, most view Jesus as a nonviolent revolutionary, but promoting forms of empowerment — particularly among the disenfranchised — that quite quickly (it seems) came to be seen as a serious threat to imperial law and order.

Jesus would have had no trials, no melodrama. The authorities seized him at an opportune moment — with or without the collusion of some of his close followers (e.g., Judas) — and proceeded to subject him to a quick and brutal death, without dignity nor mercy. And afterward, his body would have been dumped in a common pit for the wild animals to devour.[13] Perhaps we need the poet to make sense of what will feel to a lot of Christians like a demise too outrageous to entertain. How might we embrace this tragic truth without succumbing to spiritual despair?

## Redeemed through Natality, Not through Mortality!

*Salvation and redemption and the rhetoric of the Cross*
*Reveal a legacy ambivalent and strained.*
*Such a violent intervention*
*To bring about redemption*
*And remedy the friction*
*Of a postulated flaw.*
*The paschal lamb of ancient fame*
*The sacrifice to please God's name*
*Has led to centuries of devotion,*
*In a heritage many question, as we seek another way!*
*The theory of atonement reinforced redemptive lore*

With Jesus as the scapegoat to appease.
Replete with feudal imag'ry,
And quite a violent strategy
From sin we seek delivery
In death we vest all hope.
No end to suffering in sight
As if the pain could set things right.
Has led to centuries of oppression
With guilt and fear predominant in many broken hearts.

Why focus on mortality to bring about new life
With natality subverted on the way?
Empowerment for companions,
A kingdom with new passions
Embracing fresh horizons
With no one left outside.
It is in the LIFE of Jesus we are saved,
The wellspring from which all our hopes are carved.
While the brutal death Christ suffered
Was the consequence of living in bold prophetic lure.

The LIFE of Jesus paradigms our faith,
The sufferings we embrace in daily grind.
Set free from all oppression,
Strong justice in our mission,
We're risky in transgression
New vision to empower.
The call to transformation on our earth,
The hope all nations long to bring to birth.
Non-violence sets our option to be free,
As companions for empowerment transform Calvary.

There is nothing salvific or redemptive in the death of Jesus.
It was the ultimate price he paid for his radical, subversive,

empowering mission, the prospect facing every prophetic visionary. In the case of Jesus, the locus for empowerment is in his
*life,* not in his death. And it is in his life that Jesus suffers most
intensely, particularly enduring the taunts and ridicule of opponents, the misunderstandings of those whom he tried to help, and,
perhaps most bewildering of all, the dumbness and disappoint-
ment of those on whom he relied (e.g., "Do you still not perceive
or understand?" — Mark 8:17). Yes, Jesus suffered, and so will
those committed to the new Companionship created in Jesus'
name. But that suffering is in life, and for life, and not some
pseudo-mystical ideology that sanctions death and construes violent death as being somehow synonymous with salvation and
holiness.

## Atonement and Suffering

It seems to me that there is a distinct difference between the
suffering of Jesus at the service of new life (epitomized in the
Companionship of Empowerment) and the understandings of
Christian suffering that emerged over time. For instance, in the
Catacombs in Rome we find no images of a crucified Christ, nor
of a God in judgment demanding that people suffer because of
sin or wrongdoing. On the contrary, we find images celebrating
the luscious life of nature, depicting the paradise in which every
creature feels at home. Brock and Parker (2008, ix–x; 60–63)
claim that the martyrs associated with the Catacombs embraced
martyrdom, not so that they might win eternal salvation in a life
hereafter, but so that through their sufferings they would help to
bring about paradise on this earth. In other words, they did not
suffer for the sake of being redeemed through suffering; rather
they envisaged their sufferings — and their deaths — as serving a
release of new life for other persons, creatures, and creation itself.

Redemption through suffering is a historically fraught notion
and more complex than most people realize. Salvation through

the power of the Cross is assumed to be a Christian conviction that prevailed from earliest times, and already in the writings of St. Paul we find evidence for this outlook. Most church historical texts highlight martyrdom among early Christians and hail the martyrs as outstanding Christians whose holiness was exemplary precisely because they suffered so much. Suffering comes to be understood as the perennial Christian virtue, a more reliable guarantee to obtain our heavenly reward in a life hereafter.

The Cross, bearing a tortured, emaciated Christ-figure, is our permanent reminder that extreme suffering is the royal road to holiness and salvation. At least that is what many of us have been taught, and most Christians never dreamed of challenging that view. It has never dawned on us that the power of the Cross might have a deviant aspect to it, which in fact it has. In many Christian homes, churches, convents, and monasteries one is likely to see a depiction of the crucified Jesus, wearing a crown of thorns, exhausted and emaciated from intense suffering. The earliest source for that portrayal is the Gero Cross, dated 965 C.E., which can still be viewed in the cathedral of Cologne in Germany. That which we assumed was inherited in an uninterrupted way from earliest Christian times is actually quite a late development. No substantial evidence for that kind of crucifix has been found before the tenth century of the Christian era (see Brock and Parker 2008).

Prior to the tenth century, it seems that Christians more commonly used a cross with the accompanying image of *a risen, glorified Jesus,* not a tortured, emaciated one. So what brought about the change? Predominantly, two developments happening very close to each other:

(a) *1095:* Pope Urban II instructs the Crusaders that they are to wear images of a tortured, crucified Christ as they go to do battle with the infidels — presumably as a warrant for the torture of others and a validation for themselves in case they ended up being tortured.

(b) *1097:* The publication of St. Anselm's book *Cur Deus Homo?* (Why did God become human?), outlining the first formal version of what in our time has come to be known as the doctrine of the Atonement.

From this time on, suffering for the sake of suffering becomes central to the notion of Christian salvation and redemption, with the historical Jesus upheld as the paradigmatic victim, whose violent death and suffering arrested the power of sin and opened the gates of heaven for sinful creatures. And those who suffered most were the ones who stood the best chance of inheriting eternal life in heaven.

In its conventional theological meaning, atonement is essentially a dysfunctional, disempowering strategy, completely at variance with the Companionship of Empowerment. The notion of violent appeasement is born out of the feudal power system of the Middle Ages. An offended Lord must be propitiated. Restitution must be made — frequently by substitution and by scapegoating. On rare occasions the victim was another person, even one's own kin.

According to this understanding, Jesus was sent by God the father to rescue humanity from its depraved condition (sometimes named as Original Sin); hence the popular belief that Jesus came to rescue us from our sins and died to procure our salvation. Using this as his starting point, St. Anselm went on to interpret human sinfulness as a continuation of a rebellion that happened in heaven at some previous time. The rebellious angels were defeated and thrown out of heaven. Landing on earth, they began to propagate, giving birth to other sinful, rebellious creatures like themselves. To the average adult Christian in our time, it all sounds far-fetched and unreal, a lurid myth compiled by somebody with a fascination for heavenly violence.

But there is more to come. Because we are all the offspring of those rebellious angels, then we too are in continuous rebellion

against God. In the feudal culture of the Middle Ages, this translates into humans continually offending their supreme Lord, an
irresponsible behavior that deserves punishment so that repentance can follow. But the one offended in this case is the supreme,
divine God himself, in which case, argues Anselm, only one who
shares in God's own nature can fully make up to the supreme
God for humankind's rebellion.

Jesus, known as the father's beloved Son, becomes the primordial victim. Having made up to the father in a manner worthy
of divine dignity, through *obedience* and *suffering,* he (Jesus) can
now earn for humanity forgiveness of sin and the right to be
reconciled with God once more. The divine act of rescuing (the
Atonement), became synonymous with the death of Jesus on a
Cross at Golgotha. Over the centuries various commentators have
highlighted the barbaric nature of that death, which, they suggest,
makes it all the more effective in the eyes of God the father, precisely because it was cruel and barbaric. By implication the more
humans suffer on this earth, in solidarity with the sufferings of
Christ, the better their chances too of obtaining eternal salvation
with God in Heaven.

Millions still believe in the power of the Cross and in a range
of ways collude with the myth of redemptive violence. At times,
poetry can inspire and challenge us to become more critically
reflective and question dogmas that have not merely outlived their
usefulness, but should never have been taken so literally in the
first place. Adopting some insights from queer theory, the following poem invites us to outgrow our inherited soteriology and give
birth to an alternative wisdom of Gospel empowerment:

## Queering the Theory of Violent Redemption

*The Cross and Crucifixion casts a shadow so embroiled*
*With the gory details tortured like the paschal lamb of yore.*
*And the theories of atonement mid a violence sanctified*
*Beget a weird redemption for the lost and petrified.*

*The centuries' usurpation, the theories and the power,*
*The punishment of sinners, the tyrant in the sky.*
*The several distortions that weave so great a lie*
*Have long outlived their usefulness*
*And are now condemned to die.*

*According to St. Anselm, and the lure of feudal guile*
*The sinful had to suffer as judged by God on high.*
*And God demanded righteousness through a human like*
    *themselves*
*And I became the scapegoat the pact to satisfy.*
*'Twas done in love, says Abelard, to modify the fear,*
*But such a love distorted I really want to queer.*
*With patriarchal echoes, manipulating lure,*
*Has long outlived its usefulness*
*And no longer can endure.*

*All this talk about a ransom from Origen to start,*
*And Augustine picking up the violent trail.*
*Paying a ransom to the Devil like a battle of the wits,*
*Deluded by the madness which wisdom would assail.*
*And the Gospels' fascination to make me King of Jews*
*Is another cruel distortion of the truth.*
*So many violent theories, projections here abound.*
*They've long outlived their usefulness*
*And stand finally denounced.*

*I died but once upon a Cross, subversiveness aglow.*
*Empowerment in companionship drove the powers*
*To act in scare defiance, lest the masses might arise*
*And seize the power now shaking at its core.*
*My death, a consequence so mere, to make a life*
*Subversively prophetic, could not be entertained.*
*Too dangerous a memory,*
*When prophets rise with people free,*

*And life outwits the power of death*
*Even there on Calvary.*

*Even they who claim compassion for the suffering and*
      *weak,*
*Compassion with empowerment is the clue.*
*Empowering solidarity, at-one-ment in true force,*
*And those who lived in bondage saw the light!*
*But those with broad phylacteries and the power of Roman*
      *rule*
*Felt the threat of the empowerment all too bright.*
*They massacred the prophet in the panic of their doubt,*
*Knowing already seeds were sprouting*
*And subversiveness was touting*
*That the rising of the Holy One*
*Could never be subdued.*

## Beyond the Disempowering Cross

Why did Christians become so enamored with redemptive violence, and, more important, how do we now embrace the metanoia (conversion) to a more empowering way of seeing and being? We can identify at least two factors that led to the popularity of atonement spirituality. First is the sense of consolation and strength people obtain from the God who suffers, when they themselves are trapped in poverty and oppression or, on a personal level, confronted by sickness, pain, anguish, and the fear of death. The widespread appeal of Mel Gibson's *The Passion of the Christ* shows all too clearly how this lurid fascination can grip people's lives and their search for meaning when faced with the burden and anguish of meaningless suffering.

Second, and more problematic, is the tendency of all patriarchal institutions to foster co-dependency as a way of exerting control over the masses. By consistently reminding people of their sinfulness, their waywardness, and their unworthiness, it is much easier to evoke compliance and submission. When people adopt a co-dependent spirituality, they can easily be cowed into further submission by highlighting the enormity of their crime against no one less than Almighty God himself.

Fortunately, people are progressively outgrowing this dysfunctional co-dependence, although it is still far too common in the Christian world — and seems to be prevalent in other religious systems as well. Christian scholars throughout the closing decades of the twentieth century highlighted the problematic and, in fact, highly dangerous, nature of the atonement theory and its translation into redemptive violence; Brock and Parker (2008) provide one of the more incisive critiques. In the opening decade of the twenty-first century, as people struggled to make sense of a world growing more violent by the day, the theory is making something of a comeback, especially among scholars of a Girardian persuasion (e.g., Bartlett 2001; Heim 2006; *http://girardianlectionary.net/res/atonement_webpage.htm*). Translating the inherited wisdom into an idiom more congenial to our time may not be sufficient; a more radical reconstruction — honoring the primacy of the Companionship of Empowerment — seems a more authentic and compelling way to move forward.

The theology of atonement begets a spirituality of disempowerment, sometimes expressed in language like: "throwing oneself at the mercy of God." It turns God into a violent tyrant and Jesus into a victimized scapegoat. Gloating in suffering — and the mythic power of the Cross — it glamorizes pain, torture, and cruelty. In Gospel terms, God's mercy translates into the virtue of compassion. Rooted in the Greek *splangnezomai,* the compassion of Jesus, usually rendered in the Gospel text as a verb, is a strong visceral word, a stance of heart-filled solidarity with the other in its suffering, seeking to transform that same suffering into an energy for growth and transformation. Nothing condescending or patronizing in this kind of mercy!

## From Consolation to Liberation

Serious commitment to the Companionship of Empowerment requires of all Christians a radical re-evaluation of the death of Jesus and its role in opening up a better (salvific) future for humanity. A first step in that process is to revisit the life of Jesus (as distinct from his death) and at the very least resituate his death within that context. In doing that we will readily recognize that the life of Jesus, rather than his death, is where salvation and new hope are really rooted.

To this day, millions look daily at the Cross, pray to the Jesus hanging there in torture, and may even bow low in a gesture of love and worship. Why do people behave like this? In short, because it gives them a sense of comfort and consolation, particularly for those condemned to excessive pain, poverty, exploitation, and meaningless suffering of many types. Faced with this grim reality, we must be slow to judge and always open to see the heart-rending search for meaning in what I name as *the devotion of consolation.*

We must acknowledge that this excessively devotional type of spirituality does make an enormous difference to many people. It empowers them to hang on to some semblance of a meaningful life and often to survive trials and tribulations that seem to push human resourcefulness to the very limits of endurance. In this cruel, barbaric world, people need devotional outlets, not just to cope, but to be sustained in harsh times and motivated to keep on trying despite heavy odds.

Every religion has its devotional elements. Indeed, as creatures of emotion and feeling, we need such expressions of faith, which to the outsider may seem irrational, immature, and at times bizarre. Formal religion itself is weak in negotiating the integration of such devotional praxis. It tends to be dismissed as primitive or old-fashioned.

There is, and I suspect always will be, a need for the devotion of consolation. However, for Christians committed to the Companionship of Empowerment, such devotion needs to be integrated and reclaimed within a more empowering dynamic. Devotions may be consoling but they can, and often do, keep people trapped in oppression and injustice. Faced with the cruel impact of HIV/AIDS in many African countries, people cried out to the suffering Jesus on the Cross for consolation and strength, but it took the introduction of retroviral drugs to slow the deluge of premature deaths and give people some semblance of hope for the future. The drugs became available — at a manageable price — when a few drug companies transgressed international prohibitions on patents and began manufacturing at a price that poor countries could afford. It took the *pursuit of justice*, rather than the *devotion of consolation*, to inaugurate empowering hope for a different future.

In itself the devotion of consolation will never bring about systemic change and frequently will militate against it by keeping people subdued and pacified in their unjust pain and suffering. It takes liberating action to bring about the justice whereby people can reclaim dignity, value, and empowerment in their lives. This orientation I name *the spirituality of liberation* modeled on the life and ministry of the historical Jesus to the point of costing him life itself. A spirituality of liberation is congruent with the Companionship of Empowerment; the devotion of consolation in itself fails to deliver that empowering liberation Jesus desires for all people.

Unflinching commitment to the Companionship cost Jesus his earthly life in the form of an untimely brutal death. But we know that was not the end. The first followers, particularly the women, "knew" him to be alive, in fact in a way that intensified and exceeded his earthy mode of human aliveness. That extended aliveness of Jesus we describe as *the Resurrection.* It is poetry par excellence! What happened to Jesus after his earthly death, we don't know, and at one level it does not matter. My personal interest is in the transformation of the followers after the horrendous tragedy of his untimely death. They came through that experience shattered to the core, disillusioned, frightened, disbelieving and, in the case of the twelve, scattered far and wide. In time, the liberation of empowerment, worked the breakthrough.[14] And in the empowering wisdom of the Holy Spirit, first, the female followers, and much later the male ones, recommitted their lives and energy to the work of the Companionship. It is this same liberation of empowerment that made possible the conversion and transformation.

## Grieving and Empowerment

Between Calvary and Resurrection lies a liminal space in which women carry out rituals that have been largely overlooked. Kathleen Corley (2010) describes these as funerary rites, involving grieving, lament, anointing with spices, and stories of remembrance. As a grief therapist, I wish to highlight how crucial these rituals would have been to empower the women in this dark time of anguish and intense suffering. Not merely are the women sustained against such heavy odds, but they are launched into an even more bewildering space, a more intense darkness, where the first encounters with Resurrection take place. Without the grieving rituals, they might never have known the empowerment of being risen anew.

All the Gospels make clear that Resurrection in its initial awakening is a very frightening space to occupy. The old familiar world has been shattered to the core. Without the sustenance and empowerment of collective grieving, it may not be possible to negotiate this dark night of soul and senses. Poetry captures something of the paradox and breakthrough of this unique moment:

## Lament as Prophetic Protest

*The women lament, they grieve and they mourn.*
*Not just for a loved one dead and gone,*
*But for the morbid empire*
*Which crucifies the prophets,*
*And spills the blood of martyrs*
*Along the Via Dolorosa,*
*Of shattered dreams and hopes that never fade.*

*The women lament, they grieve and they mourn.*
*Making public the subverted pain.*
*The torture that subdues,*
*Yet never eliminates life nor truth.*
*The subversive hope for freedom,*
*Awaiting the first sunrise of an Easter morning,*
*Amid the wailing cries to set the people free.*

*The women lament, they grieve and mourn.*
*Unlocking the crippling power*
*Of grief that's buried deep inside.*
*Those who refuse to shed tears,*
*The stiff upper lip of make-believe,*
*Imprisons the pain that knows how to resist*
*And will resist, whatever be the cost.*

*The women lament, they grieve and they mourn.*
*The language of the heart, broken yet released.*
*The lonely cry of deliverance*
*That shatters the deadly silence,*
*Irrupting in a dirge evoking hope.*
*The women stand, lamentation will not budge,*
*Till the piercing light of truth illuminates the dark.*

## Risen Hope for the Future

Resurrection, I suggest, is the icing on the cake for a life radically lived. It is God's ultimate vindication of the Companionship of Empowerment. Angelic figures, empty tomb scenarios, and various appearances create the metanarrative that empowered early Christian ecclesiology and gave hope and meaning to Christians especially in times of hardship and persecution. However, the glamour and rarity of those events can grossly distract us from the primary goal of Christian faith, which must never prioritize supernatural power from afar for hopeless, passive sinners. Rather faith must prioritize the empowerment born out of the relational matrix of a prophetic person whose life-and-death was totally devoted to the Companionship of Empowerment. Only when Christians, and others, take that seriously do we stand any realistic hope of realizing in our own lives what the mystery and meaning of Resurrection are all about. It is God's vindication of the beloved ones when we work unstintingly to realize God's Kingdom in our earthly, cosmic home. (For a fine overview of contemporary thinking on the Resurrection, see Pagola 2009, 387–406.)

Faithfulness to the Companionship of Empowerment requires of every Christian our primary commitment to *the liberation of empowerment*. While we acknowledge and seek to integrate the devotion of consolation, we must ensure that it never hinders our commitment to justice and liberation in the name of Gospel empowerment.

We need consoling forms of spirituality not as ends in themselves, but to empower us to confront the injustices that undermine life (at every level), and to work unceasingly for the transformation that reinforces growth and development for all. It is not good enough to look up at the Cross and plead to God for mercy; rather the Cross must inspire us to look beyond it and unite our efforts in ridding our world of every Cross that imperial domination has invented, and help re-create our world in justice, peace, and nonviolent hope for a better future.

Christian redemption inspired by the Companionship of Empowerment is not about some heroic deed the historical Jesus once achieved. It is about the Christ in the relational body of contemporary Christians working zealously for justice and freedom for all — even to the point of giving our lives in the process. And when the Christian people make a more unanimous, overt commitment to this ideal, then we will know experientially what Resurrection means: the radical new hope of God alive in our midst.

# Chapter Nine

# Liberating Jesus
# from Colonial Mimicry

*We have received from the Divine Providence the supreme favor of being relieved from all error.*     — CONSTANTINE

*Theology has been growing uncertain for centuries. Therein lies its great opportunity.*     — CATHERINE KELLER

Liberation theology in its heyday sought to champion the poor and marginalized as God's specially chosen people. Jesus himself was set among the poor and portrayed as one who intimately knew and understood the plight of the poor and disenfranchised. And the Jewish tradition out of which Jesus emerged was often interpreted against the background of the Exodus story, as God leads the people to the promised land of new hope and freedom.

Liberation theology itself — like much liberationist thinking throughout the latter half of the twentieth century — was the birthchild of theologians mainly formed in Western imperial theology. Many were aware of this context and tried to outgrow it, yet to varying degrees it remained a bind that hindered and impeded the liberty and freedom that was proclaimed by a mere handful of Christian scholars but sought by millions living in poverty, degradation, and oppression. In not a few cases, a clash of ideologies began to emerge, particularly from a Catholic hierarchy still entrenched in the imperial fortress of Roman defiance.

Anything that smacked of a political gospel was considered suspect, and the dangerous memory of the subversively liberating Jesus was once more subverted.

Liberation theology proved to be the most popular and widely known of new theological developments in the latter decades of the twentieth century. Feminism, black theology, multifaith dialogue, and creation theology (new cosmology) were among some of the other developments stretching the horizons of theological engagement. All were seeking to expand theological engagement beyond the patriarchal restrictions that favored the white Western imperial mind-set. Central to all these new developments was a desire to reframe the power basis of Christian faith and shift the foundations from the patriarchal hegemony to a more egalitarian and empowering endeavor. Millions of rank-and-file Christians began to share the new enthusiasm, while church authority in general resisted and, at times, denounced these newly emerging trends.

The liberation of theology from its patriarchal moorings has been an enterprise of mixed fortunes as can be seen in the growth and development of liberation theology. With hindsight one begins to wonder if instead of the oft-cited criticism of "going too far" its foundational weakness is that it did not go far enough. Now with the emergence of the postcolonial critique, gathering momentum in the early twenty-first century, we seem to have a resource that names the critical issues with greater clarity, discerns the historical baggage with greater depth, and provides a more prophetic strategy for change and transformation.

## The Postcolonial Vision

This new vision, with its complex implications, is outlined by Fernando Segovia and R. S. Sugirtharajah in a set of essays on the postcolonial New Testament (Segovia and Sugirtharajah 2009). The essays highlight imagery and language that challenges and even denounces the prevailing imperial order (especially of Rome) but, time and again, reinscribes its core values in the alternative vision of the Christian scriptures. The Kingdom of Rome was replaced with the Kingdom of God as an alternative vision, with bold new possibilities for freedom and hope. Under Constantine, however, a radical reversal took place, which Christians of the time were not capable of either acknowledging or resisting (for the greater part). The old imperial consciousness still held its grip on people's imaginations.

In fact, long before Constantine, the duplicity had taken root. Borg and Crossan (2009) depict how Paul's radically inclusive vision was compromised by those interpreting what he said and did. Nor can Paul himself be exonerated from colluding with the imperial attitudes and values that prevailed all around him.

The Gospels, too, are influenced by the culture of power and domination, often depicting Jesus in something of a double bind. Kathleen Corley (2002) concurs broadly with the feminist tendency to affirm Jesus' positive regard for women, yet it is often done with imagery and language from the inherited imperial culture, e.g., repeating the derogatory term "harlots" in the allusion to those who enter the Kingdom (Matt. 21:31–32). We can never be sure of course whether this was the historical Jesus speaking, or using words attributed to him by the Gospel writers who were clearly influenced by the dominant culture of the time. And even among the Gospel writers, John seems to be more enculturated in patriarchal lore and values than the Synoptic writers.

All this leaves us with the daunting question that is the focus of the present chapter: How do we liberate Jesus from the shackles of inherited patriarchal indoctrination? How do we revision the life and ministry of the historical Jesus so that we honor the priority of the Companionship of Empowerment, which seems to have been the foundational basis for everything Jesus said and did? More formidable still, how do we decolonize Jesus of Aristotelian individualized personhood so that he can become once more the catalyst for the communal model suggested in chapter 2 above? And how do we move beyond so much biblical literalism that circumvents and undermines archetypal truths that help us to access a more empowering Christ — within the Gospels themselves and as an object of faith for contemporary seekers after Christian truth?

Two issues seem to be confused for much of the two-thousand-year Christian era. First, there is the cultural construction of the human Jesus, portrayed as a person of power and status, similar to the ideal male projection of the prevailing patriarchal culture. Second, there is Jesus the archetype of humanity fully alive (see Wink 2002). As an archetype, this Jesus belongs to the transhistorical and transcultural realm — embodying human potentials belonging to all times, cultures, and religions. However, the archetype also includes vulnerability and fragility, human weakness, and the capacity to make mistakes. Without these dimensions the archetype is incomplete, and the radical humanity of Jesus cannot serve as an authentic gateway to manifest the divine and the transcendent.

Throughout the Gospels, Jesus becomes the victim of colonial mimicry. On the one hand Jesus is portrayed as the antidote to Roman imperialism; on the other hand, his life-story is often modeled on the prevailing values of that same system. This is particularly so in John's Gospel with Jesus himself claiming to be a King. Similarly, the archetypal vision embodied in the notion of the Kingdom of God is also compromised and subverted, with earthly kingship assumed to be the basic model to be adopted — exactly what Gelarius and Constantine did about three hundred years later. The Aramaic rendering of the Kingdom of God as the Companionship for Empowerment gets lost not merely in translation, but also in the colonial mimicry, the transliteration of earthly kingship into the mission and vision of Jesus.

Volumes have been written about the various titles attributed to Jesus in the Gospels. Many commentators view these positively as affirmations of the divine transcendence of Jesus and indicate that such titles may have entered the Gospels having been adopted from liturgical contexts where they were initially used — to praise and glorify God (or Jesus). Others are more reticent, suggesting that the only title Jesus may have applied to himself was that of *the Son of Man,* which is often translated as the Human One, but worthy of note are its communal connotations detectable in some of the parallels in the Hebrew scriptures. Postcolonial scholars are quick to point out that many of the titles attributed to Jesus were also used as appellations for Roman emperors, raising further doubts about their authenticity as self-designations used by Jesus and requiring a more thorough investigation on what might have motivated the Gospel writers to adopt such titles. All of this leads us to share the sense of bewilderment articulated by Maia Kotrosits when she wrote:

> There is not an uncomplicated mention of Jesus' identity in the entire Gospel. There are indeed multiple identifications used for Jesus at various times with no clear distinctions about their use, from the fairly straightforward address "Rabbi," to the highly ambiguous self-declaration "son of Adam/son of Man," to the apparently related terms "son of David" and "Anointed," not to mention the indications of Jesus as God's son. For as often as Jesus is titled and called, it seems Mark does not know exactly what to call him. (Quoted by Taussig 2009, 187)

## Mark's Gospel

Mark's Gospel is considered to be the oldest of the Synoptic writings, the basis on which Matthew and Luke develop their narratives. Many of the leading scholars of postcolonialism (Ched Myers, Herman C. Waetjen, Benny Liew, Mary Ann Tolbert) identify a range of imperial motifs in Mark's version of the

Jesus story. These include: (a) a tendency to attribute absolute authority to Jesus; (b) reinscribing the insider-outsider binary opposition; (c) consistently modeling legitimate authority on that of the prevailing patriarchal prototype.

Benny Liew (1999) goes so far as to describe Jesus in the Markan account as a master scribe who enjoys tyrannical authority to interpret, change, or break scripture. Consistently Jesus is portrayed as Lord of the community, who authorizes his servants and commands his doorkeeper to keep watch (Mark 13:34–37). He favors a clear preference for insiders, condemning all others to be outsiders. While Mark seems to be focused on undermining imperial Roman power, he actually adopts a might-is-right ideology, thus mimicking the very dispensation he is seeking to undermine.

In terms of speaking truth to power, I find it necessary to ask Benny Liew whose Jesus is he describing: the Jesus of history (insofar as we can get access to him) or Mark's portrayal of Jesus? This, of course, is the great hermeneutical question that some scholars try to dismiss as both irresponsible or irrelevant, countering that the only Jesus we can get access to is the Jesus portrayed by the Gospel writers: "Jesus remembered," to adopt the language of James G. Dunn (2003). And yet, a range of contemporary studies, in the social scientific sphere, require us to grapple precisely with this question, acknowledging that:

(a) the portrayal of Jesus in the four Gospels differs significantly on several points;

(b) the reliance of the Synoptic writers on the Q source, their use and interpretation of Q, is still very much under investigation;

(c) the Roman attack of 66–70 C.E. seems to have impacted strongly on how Mark wrote his Gospel, influencing particularly the apocalyptic flavor, also adopted by the other Synoptic writers;

(d) by the time the Gospels came to be written — at least
thirty years after the death of Jesus — ecclesiastical law
and regulation were exerting a strong influence. We detect
this in several of the early letters of Paul, and we can
see it at work in a text like Matthew 22:1–14 where in
the name of the inclusive vision of the Companionship
of Empowerment people of every background are invited
to the wedding feast; the host (king) comes along and
expels one person because he is not properly clothed, thus
highlighting an insider-outsider distinction, which, in all
probability, does not belong to the primordial tradition of
the Companionship of Empowerment.

I concur with the postcolonial analysts that there are indeed
examples in the Gospels of colonial mimicry — both in the behavior of Jesus and in that of others associated with him. And
yet, I detect in the complex symbol of the Companionship of
Empowerment (the Kingdom) a fundamental layer of truth, with
radical inclusiveness and empowerment at its core, marking an
unambiguous shift from all semblance of colonial patriarchal
power. The colonial echoes, therefore, we encounter in the Gospels belong either to the Gospel writers (rather than to Jesus) or
may be explained as mistakes made by the historical Jesus, due
to the limitations of his human nature.

## Could Jesus Be Mistaken?

That Jesus could get things wrong and make mistakes as other
humans do is intolerable language for millions of Christians. It
is simply unthinkable! As a divine person, it is widely assumed
that he was perfect, all-knowing, all-powerful, beyond the capacity to make mistakes. But how can we claim that Jesus was
fully human if we eliminate any possibility of making mistakes?
Presumably as a full human being he internalized the values of

his day as most other people did. And as a human being, he
would have erred at times; otherwise we cannot claim that he was
authentically human. Making mistakes is *an essential ingredient*
of genuine human-ness. In many ways the emphasis on divinity
has obfuscated the fuller meaning of Jesus' true humanity.

Here we evidence postcolonial influence in one of its more
sinister forms. Religion throughout human history has had a special appeal for peoples who were oppressed and subjugated. In
patriarchal cultures particularly, the gods of formal religion are
popularly perceived as divine rescuers with an omniscience and
omnipotence totally unknown to humans. Millions of people over
the centuries have internalized this passive acquiescence to an all-
powerful divine rescuer. And with this passive acceptance comes
the naïve, unexamined assumption that God is beyond all human
limitation and can never make a mistake. Essentially, it is a God-
image born out of human oppression, the very thing, I contend,
that Jesus came to overthrow.

The Companionship of Empowerment is not just about a new
way of humans feeling empowered by God; it is based on a radically new understanding of who and what God is. As I indicate
in chapter 2, this is another area in which the Gospel writers
got it badly wrong. They clung on to the notion that Jesus as a
representative of God had to be king-like in his essential nature,
imbued with divine imperial power, which he would have lov-
ingly and willingly inherited from his Jewish religious culture. I
favor the line put forward by Thomas Sheehan (1986) that in all
probability Jesus sought to outgrow all religious allegiance — and
I wish to add, all patriarchal allegiance — inviting people instead
to embrace the godliness within and around them in the ordinar-
iness of their daily lives and in the mutual empowerment they
would facilitate for each other through love and justice. This is
Christian incarnation at its true core.

In that incarnational realm a Jesus incapable of making mistakes would simply be a fake. He would not embody the fullness

of humanity that God seeks to call forth in all people, a humanity in process, growing, evolving, unfolding, getting it wrong sometimes, and ideally learning from mistakes as we go along. But if the prevailing religious culture does not want to acknowledge the value of mistakes in the first place, how can we ever hope to learn from them?

We come therefore to a favorite example of postcolonial critique, the story of the Syro-Phoenician woman (Mark 7:24–30; Matt. 15:21–28). Scholars such as Jim Perkinson (1996) describe this as a classic example of Jesus submerged in a postcolonial quagmire, seeking to dismiss the woman with the colonized derogatory language of a Gentile dog, and arrogantly asserting that his liberation is only for the true Jewish people. I find a far more compelling discernment in the view that this is an all-too-human Jesus making a dreadful error — almost unforgiveable in terms of the Companionship of Empowerment.

As we enter the story in that way, we begin to see the Companionship break through with incredible vigor and vitality. Despite the ideological assertiveness of Jesus' statement, the woman does not succumb, bow her head in shame, and walk away. No, to the contrary, she challenges Jesus forthrightly, using his own words, and in an articulation with many echoes of subversive poetry, denounces what Jesus is doing, but goes on to call forth in him a new liberation and recommitment to his primary task as the herald of the new Reign of God in the world. The whole episode glows in poetic possibility:

## Persistent Inclusiveness

*I'm known as the woman from Syrophoenecia,*
*A mole in the system of God's chosen race.*
*Even Jesus fell foul and tried to exclude me*
*From the specially chosen of God's divine grace.*
*He even suggested derogatory status,*

*The pagans like dogs so often described.*
*But my faith is dogged, persistent and fiery,*
*Outwitting the dogmas in religion prescribed.*

*I'm known as the woman from Syrophoenecia,*
*And my family call me Ranana by name.*
*Long blessed with the gift of wise intuition,*
*I know what goes on in the patriarch's game.*
*I won't be fobbed off even by a Messiah*
*And I won't give the Jews every right that they claim.*
*Though I eat the mere crumbs from beneath the table,*
*I'm nourished by God with the fruit of the grain.*

*I'm known as the woman from Syrophoenecia,*
*My daughter distressed from internalized pain.*
*And I know it would take just the crumbs of inclusion*
*To restore her spirit, her health to regain.*
*But entering battle for what we're entitled*
*In the name of empowerment in justice and love!*
*When all can be named and called forth in wholeness,*
*Dogmatic exclusions we'll one day resolve!*

*A new Reign of God, empowerment for all,*
*The rumors have stirred in my soul.*
*And I'll never give up till the dream has come true,*
*A vision embracing us all!*

(also see "A Woman's Dogged Faith" in O'Murchu 2009, 151–52)

Yes, Jesus made many mistakes in his lifetime. Like Paul, he expected some dramatic end to history in his lifetime — and was patently wrong! On the Cross, he cried out in a language of despair. Where does that leave the omnipotent God? We cannot be sure of the historical accuracy of these examples, but they are consistent with that all-too-human Jesus, the radical face of Holy Wisdom in our midst.

There are other, more complex examples, which carry a subversive meaning that may have been intended rather than delivered in error. For instance, the text in Mark 2:23–26:

> One the sabbath he was going through the grainfields; and as they made their way his disciples began to pluck ears of grain. And the Pharisees said to him: "Look, why are they doing what is not lawful on the sabbath?" And he said to them: "Have you never read what David did, when he was in need and was hungry, he and those who were with him: how he entered the house of God, when Abiathar was high priest, and ate the bread of the Presence, which it is not lawful for any but the priests to eat, and also gave to those who were with him." And he said to them, "The sabbath was made for man, not man for the sabbath; so the Son of man is lord even of the sabbath." (RSV)

This passage is full of textual errors, to such an extent that the opponents would have had material to turn Jesus into a complete laughingstock, such are the interpretative blunders he makes in this narrative. Gundry (1993, 141) identifies seven misinterpretations of the foundational text of 1 Samuel 21:1–7, the chief errors being: David had no companions with him; David does not enter the house of God (see next verse); the priest is Ahimelech, not Abiathar; and neither David nor his companions ate the bread of presence.

Is this Jesus making a massive blunder, exhibiting a distinctive ignorance of his faith tradition, or might it be, as William Herzog (2000, 188) suggests, that Jesus identifies with "David the fugitive, the coyote figure who lives by his wits while others are seeking to destroy him. This is a David figure who would be appreciated in the villages." There are examples in the Gospels where Jesus seems to be calling people's bluff, but beneath the ironic humor, and perhaps some poetic liberty with inherited truth-tradition, is the call to a radical shift in perspective, and the need to outgrow old allegiances in favor of the new dispensation breaking open in their midst.

Once more we may be on more authentic ground as we hear the poet unravel the complexities and paradoxes of what seems to be a poetic parable rather than anything resembling standard prose:

### Stretching the Subversive Imagination

*How do we speak subversive truth*
*And how do we undermine?*
*And run the risk of a laughing stock*
*When we venture to opine.*
*Distort the facts to make a plea,*
*Take sacred text so lightly,*
*Is this the prophetic paradox*
*Resolving truth so blithely?*

*According to Samuel 21,*
*David eludes the truth.*
*Claiming he was working for Saul*
*When in fact he was being pursued*
*And Jesus devises a conjured plot:*
*David raids the temple store*
*As if he was hungry and needed food*
*Not stated in scripture lore.*

*According to Samuel 21,*
*David was on his own.*
*Without the others the Gospel names*
*With whom he shared the loan.*
*A fugitive of coyote skill*
*Outwitting those in hot pursuit,*
*Surviving the games of fortune lost*
*Despite the cost to his own repute.*

*And the little people would resonate*
*With this trickster to survive.*
*A parable rare we need to hear*
*Oppressed but still will thrive.*
*How do we interpret sacred lore*
*A new dream to empower?*
*Subversive wisdom is tricky stuff*
*With a logic as strange as a winter flower.*

## Reclaiming Vulnerability

Colonial consciousness tends to be dismissive of people who make mistakes. They are the weak ones we need to get rid of, since colonialism of all types flourishes on the survival of the fittest. Consequently, the colonial mind-set will be reluctant to attribute qualities to God or to Jesus that resemble too closely the human reality. One of the big fears is that we might go further and insinuate that Jesus also committed sin, as other humans do, and then the icon of the all-good, perfect God is essentially shattered to pieces. Vulnerability has gone too far!

Can vulnerability ever go too far in terms of the radical compassion which is a key quality of life in the Companionship of Empowerment? The work of empowerment is through vulnerability, weakness, mistakes, and sinfulness, not in spite of them. This is vividly expressed in Luke 7:47 in the encounter between Jesus and the woman with the alabaster jar; it is the one who has sinned who knows how to receive forgiveness and with it the new liberation to love much.

In this context, "compassion" also becomes quite a subversive — and empowering — word. Scripture scholar Marcus Borg employs the word in all his major writings, making the bold claim that for Jesus the politics of purity is to be replaced by the politics of compassion (Borg 1994b, 58). Imperial holiness required allegiance to ritual codes, which many of the poor and marginalized could never fulfill. It left many people weighed down by unworthiness, guilt, and disempowerment. In the new dispensation, it is to be replaced by an embracing, empowering love that must transcend all the labels of exclusion and inferiority:

> The central quality of the community of Jesus can be seen in the paradigm or core value that was meant to shape its life. The dominant paradigm structuring his social world was: "Be holy as God is holy" (Lev. 19:2), with holiness understood as purity. Jesus echoed this passage even as he deliberately contrasted it by substituting compassion: "Be compassionate as God is compassionate" (Luke 6:36)....
> Concern with purity intrinsically creates boundaries; the life of compassion intrinsically reaches across boundaries. Like the Spirit of whom compassion is the primary fruit, compassion shatters boundaries. In short the Jesus movement was a community of compassion, and to take Jesus seriously means to become part of such a community. (Borg 1994a, 154)

The Companionship of Empowerment shatters all boundaries. There is neither top nor bottom, insider nor outsider, patron nor client. All dualisms are collapsed, all derogatory labels are suppressed, hierarchies are to be replaced by holarchies, and only a love that takes justice seriously can be taken seriously. This is the crucial distinction between discipleship in the Companionship as distinct from conventional Christianity. Mainline Christian faith places an enormous emphasis on love, but it is often a sentimental feeling, based on being nice to others and treating them gently and without offense. This is not Gospel-based love which is often fierce and passionate, challenging and empowering, seeking reform and transformation of every oppressive and disempowering system. Without a radical commitment to justice, human love can be dangerously patronizing and disempowering. It has little to contribute to living authentically in the new Companionship.

## Beyond Colonial Perfection

The forces of colonization tend to leave behind them a trail of internalized oppression that can take centuries to outgrow. In such a regime one is never good enough, unless one capitulates totally to the invading power and becomes a kind of cultural zombie. Colonizers dread even the slightest challenge to their power and hegemony. They may claim to be empowering people by importing the luring goods of the dominant culture, as transnational corporations often do today in poorer nations, but increasingly this is a camouflage that people see through and refuse to collude with it. As people become more educated and informed, the mechanism of mimicry no longer works.

Postcolonial analysis certainly serves to expose power games and dynamics that dominant cultures tend to hide or subvert. And in what is still a patriarchally inundated culture, we all need to be conscientized to the allurement of false power and how quickly we can capitulate to its seductiveness. The goal, however, must be one of honoring complexity and ambiguity rather than some new type of perfectionism that could become yet another ideology.

Unexpected events in the life of the historical Jesus may indeed bear the brunt of colonial infiltration, but they can also be genuine human mistakes of someone who was fully human and can only serve for humanity as an authentic revelation of human fullness, wherein errors, and even deviations, are included. Colonialism cannot tolerate mistakes and colonizers tend to be severe in the punishments they administer. This is the violent way to impose order and control, but certainly not the way to liberating justice. The nonviolent strategy, which is often one of learn as you go along and learn particularly from one's mistakes, is much more akin to Gospel liberation and to the life-example that the historical Jesus has left to his followers.

On that note I want to end the reflections of this chapter with poetic echoes of how Jesus himself might wish to reassure his followers, challenging them too to embrace and transform their mistakes rather than denying and suppressing them.

## Incarnational Mistakes

*Of course, I made mistakes — I had no other choice,*
*The price of being so human, through and through.*
*That the world soon would end,*
*That God's judgment would descend,*
*Jewish preference defend.*
*And sometimes I realized what a struggle 'twould entail*
*To be faithful to the dream of an earthly paradise.*

*The patriarchal dominance was a nightmare to engage,*
*It left me feeling like a loser from the start.*
*messianic power inflate,*
*Male examples dominate,*
*Slurs on women perforate.*
*Thank God, I had the mountain when I needed to escape,*
*Struggling to maintain the pace, precarious the dream.*

*The women I embraced, defying my culture and my race,*
*Yet, I genderized the culture's flavored plot.*
*The women were included,*
*But their presence well secluded,*
*Forgive me — I colluded.*
*And that woman of dogged faith who righteously did not*
     *renege*
*Left me shaking with embarrassment for many days ahead.*

*Two thousand years of history and the problem still remains,*
*Embracing Incarnation in full scope.*
*Divinity the culprit,*
*Misleading and corrupted,*
*Humanity co-opted*

*In the patriarchal power games, projected make-believe,*
*Subverting God's uniqueness in my sheer humanity.*

*You can't be truly human unless you make mistakes.*
*Revelation's mighty paradox,*
*Incarnation's unrelenting crux.*
*Neglect not the mistakes you make:*
*God gets it wrong as well!*

## Chapter Ten

# Is an Empowering
# Church Possible?

*Forget about the local church as the paradigm of the Chris-*
*tian community. The principle of two or three gathering*
*together still holds firm. But the gathering is simply the high*
*velocity acceleration of the force field of radical relationality.*
— CARL RASCHKE

*In an increasingly globalized world, models matter more*
*than ever. If the map does not fit the territory, we cannot*
*navigate the perilous currents surrounding us.*
— MARC C. TAYLOR

The Christian churches have largely neglected the prophetic
cutting edge for which Jesus lived and died. This leaves growing numbers of Christians feeling distrustful of, and ambiguous
toward, all Christian institutions, churches in particular. Many
more informed Christians prefer to explore a fresh sense of their
faith outside rather than within ecclesiastical contexts. Hopefully,
this book will be a valuable resource for such seekers.

Any church or religious institution that wishes to serve humanity in a more empowering way must ensure that its theology
(vision) is solidly grounded in the Companionship of Empowerment. Christian theology has often failed in this regard, and so has
ecclesiology, bequeathing an ecclesial lifeline that failed to liberate or empower millions of Christians. In order to avoid repeating

past mistakes the following guidelines seem to be essential for a healthier and hope-filled future:

- Jesus remains emblematic and prophetic for contemporary Christians not because he was a faithful religious devotee, but because he prophetically calls people to a fullness of life that transcends all religion and overtly denounces the dynamics of power upon which a great deal of formal religion is based.

- The prophetic strategy adopted by Jesus is that of the Kingdom of God, which needs to be reclaimed under the more inclusive, empowering rendering of the original Aramaic: *The Companionship of Empowerment.*

- In this new vision all forms of patriarchal power are denounced and revisioned. Empowerment (signifying power-with), rather than the control of power (power over), is the primary dream and strategy adopted by Jesus.

- And the word "companionship" is also crucial, signifying that Jesus does not even support benign empowerment from the top down. No, all empowerment must be born out of a new value-base of mutuality, symbolized primarily in the open common table (commensality). All power pyramids are declared redundant; only circles of empowerment are appropriate.

- This shift from power-over to mutual empowerment involves liberation from all forms of oppression, marginalization, disenfranchisement. The standard procedures for political and economic engagement are heavily critiqued, and in this process the dualism between the sacred and the secular becomes irrelevant.

- The prophetic conscientization is facilitated through provocative story-telling and subversive imagination. The parables turn the conventional world upside-down and pose an enormous challenge to the normativity of linear logic, rational discourse, and hierarchical structures.

• Walter Brueggemann's claim that the prophetic will-to-meaning is rooted in the power of the symbolic is illustrated in the Gospel's miracle tradition and particularly in the complex metaphorical interplay with demonic forces (see chapter 1 above). Our pursuit of a supernatural explanation for the miracles seriously distracts from their prophetic, symbolic import as rituals for healing and empowerment (see chapter 5 above).

• Contrary to our inherited Christian tradition, God's saving power (salvation, redemption, etc.) is facilitated primarily through his life and not through his death on the Cross. His untimely death was a consequence of his radical prophetic dedication to "the fullness of life" (cf. John 10:10). Resurrection then can be seen as God's ultimate vindication of a life radically lived rather than being in any way connected with his death (see chapter 7).

Many of these ideas coalesce in this summary quotation:

The deliberate conjunction of magic and meal, miracle and table, free compassion and open commensality, was a challenge launched not just at Judaism's strictest purity regulations or even at the Mediterranean's patriarchal combination of honor and shame, patronage and clientage, but at civilization's eternal inclination to draw lines, invoke boundaries, establish hierarchies, and maintain discriminations. It did not invite a political revolution but envisaged a social one at the imagination's most dangerous depths. (Crossan 1991, xii)

## Unmasking the Power

For a long time, Christians have been making interpretative choices that are no longer sustainable. We have evaded some central truths that now need to be reclaimed, and the process is already well under way, although largely ignored (and sometimes despised) by church officialdom. The retrieval taking place belongs to scripture scholars and theologians from within the sphere of academic scholarship and research, but also to a growing body of critical creative thinkers from within the wider Christian community.

Speaking truth to power is a daunting enterprise. Centuries of tradition, accumulations of laws, layers of customs that over time have morphed into ideologies, institutions, dogmas, and doctrines — all developed to safeguard the truth of power often at the expense of the power of truth. Every major religion gained cultural supremacy because in its primordial vision it cut through inherited ideologies and made radiant a new spiritual awakening with more direct access to the light of enduring truth. This, I suggest, is what Jesus achieved in his unflinching allegiance to the Companionship of Empowerment.

Jesus rattled the certainties of his day. He questioned truths nobody dared to doubt and subverted procedures couched in divine law. He broke rank with those who expected his allegiance and fidelity and befriended those disenfranchised by the power-mongering of the day. In doing all that not merely was he deconstructing an ideological edifice; more importantly, he was rekindling a kind of primal spiritual force that underpins all religion and predates formal religion by thousands of years. What made Jesus authentically messianic was not some direct access to the God described as "father" in John's Gospel, but rather a deep attunement with the Holy Spirit, the source of all life and animation throughout the entire web of creation. In the empowerment of the Spirit, symbolized in baptism, Jesus is declared to be God's Beloved!

In the language and liturgy of the Christian churches one rarely hears the word "empowerment!" And while the word "community" tends to be used extensively, it fails to encapsulate the sense of partnership and egalitarianism denoted by the notion of "companionship." Power is often invoked, mainly as an attribute of God, as in the phrase "the power of the Holy Spirit." On closer examination, however, we note that God is portrayed as powerful because humans are — and always will be — powerless. God's power is essentially a redemptive power through which sinful humans can be rescued and redeemed.

For most churches, empowerment is a strange word. But more to the point, it is a dangerously disconcerting word. Organizationally, churches may boast about pastoral councils, consultative bodies, and delegation of authority, but in all cases it is unambiguously clear where the buck stops: with the parish pastor, the bishop, or a member of the ecclesiastical hierarchy at a more elevated level. Empowerment of others is acceptable as long as everyone is clear about the chain of command, and all acknowledge the one in whom authority and power are finally invested.

Empowerment has strong connotations of giving power away, passing on wisdom and skill, so that the people of God become the church they were always intended to be. A noble aspiration indeed, but little evidence for its existence in the landscape of modern Christianity.

## Disposing Inherited Baggage

In chapter 1, I alluded to Brueggemann's double take on prophetic vision: the dual task of criticizing and energizing, or more accurately, criticism in order to energize. In some of the Christian churches, criticism is still viewed as irreverent, unbecoming, disrespectful, indicating a lack of faithfulness to one degree or another.

In general, patriarchal institutions tend to be fearful of and antagonistic toward most forms of critique and analysis. It is okay to call others to repentance and conversion, but the church itself, despite the rhetoric of "ecclesia semper reformanda" (a church always seeking reform), feels somewhat above all that. Others, rather than itself, are to blame for its limitations and failures.

A growing body of more informed and enlightened Christians is increasingly being alienated by the church's tendency to hold on to trappings of the past. These include the following:

## 1. Patriarchal Power

That the pope is a political head of state (the Vatican) feels to many like a total betrayal of the Jesus who had nowhere to lay his head. This status entitles the pope to all sorts of exemptions and privileges, which seem to mark a serious departure from the key values of the Kingdom of God. Other Christian denominations also tend to model their supreme leaders on ancient royal protocol, indicating a widespread lack of understanding of the anti-imperial dynamic that characterizes the Companionship of Empowerment.

## 2. A Eurocentric Worldview

Today, an estimated 80 percent of Christians live outside mainland Europe, and in terms of regular practice, Europe exhibits one of the lowest rates anywhere in the world. Yet, on closer examination, the universal, non-European church is still heavily inculturated in European-based structure, custom, legalism, ritual (liturgy), and tradition. Despite a concerted effort throughout the latter half of the twentieth century to pursue inculturation in Africa, Latin America, and Asia, all the Christian churches still exhibit ways of organizing, praying, and relating which belong to their European inheritance. And in some of the Christian churches, genuine attempts at inculturation, e.g., in liturgy or morality, have either been discouraged or in some cases openly frowned upon.

## 3. A Cultural Fixation on the Past

One reason why inculturation has proved so difficult is an assumption, often unarticulated, that what we have inherited from the past has somehow stood the test of time and must be deemed better than the present. A strange kind of ideology seems to be at work here. For instance, in Catholicism, once a matter of faith has been defined doctrinally, it can never be abrogated — despite the fact that cultural conditions have radically changed. According to the Council of Trent in the sixteenth century, the number of sacraments was formally declared to be *seven,* with the added emphasis that there can never be more or less. Such stipulations contradict the universal process of evolutionary growth and development, and in an age of mass information, this quality of allegiance to the past makes the church sound archaic and irrelevant to many Christians.

## 4. A Rhetoric of Tedium

I borrow this phrase from the moral theologian Mark D. Jordan (2000), commenting on the Catholic Church's excessive moralistic rhetoric on sexual matters. Official church documents frequently exhibit a ponderous, metaphysical style of writing and vocabulary, very different from Gospel narrative, characterized by the wit and wisdom of parabolic lore. Even Christians versed in ecclesiastical language and familiar with church processes often find the language incomprehensible and alienating. The body of the faithful rarely have direct access to, or little interest in, such formal teachings. They often learn of them through sensational media reporting, compounding a kind of cynicism toward official church teachings, which is already quite widespread. All of this suggests that the church as a channel for communicating Good News is failing rather dismally in its task.

## 5. Clinging to a Dualistic Worldview

Early Christianity borrowed heavily from Greek philosophy and continues to do so even to our time. This is particularly noticeable in the liberal use of dualistic binary distinctions. While a great deal of the emerging spirituality of the twentieth and twenty-first centuries seeks to build bridges across the divide between the sacred and the secular, body and soul, matter and spirit, church and state? denominational spiritualities rarely move in this direction. Clinging to this inherited, and now largely discredited, philosophy causes serious obstacles to interfaith dialogue and even more to the adoption of a multidisciplinary strategy in addressing the major problems confronting humankind — and the living earth — today.

## 6. Religious Exclusivity

In our highly globalized world, it seems incredible to many Christians that the churches can still be so sectarian in their attempts to protect what they deem to be uniquely theirs. There seems to be a huge preoccupation to preserve and safeguard differences and little serious discernment around commonalities. This is indeed strange, and certainly not prophetic in a world so brutally divided politically and economically. In this climate, creative dialogue among the different religions becomes hazardous, as Christians get knotted up in theological niceties about the uniqueness of Jesus and the uniqueness of Christian faith. Of course, uniqueness is not the issue; *superiority is,* a false naming that growing numbers of Christians recognize all too readily.

## 7. Strong on Charity but Weak on Justice

Critics like myself are often accused of ignoring or bypassing the wonderful works of mercy and charity in which all the Christian churches have excelled over the centuries. Charity can be deceptively alluring to both those dispensing it and those at the receiving end. The feel-good factor can be highly deceptive. The tendency to patronize can be subtle, and on the part of the recipients the felt need to return loyalty can be entrapping. Justice is the safety valve that prevents charity from being abusive. Combined with justice, charity can become empowering rather than patronizing. And while charity focuses on people and their human needs, justice embraces the much more complex systemic issues that charity on its own tends to ignore. Justice rather than charity is the primary characteristic of the Companionship of Empowerment, and its outreach is not merely personal or interpersonal, but systemic, economic, political, and ecological. Today the Christian church struggles to embrace this enlarged vision.

## Poetic Interlude

Moving from a critique of the church in its prevailing — and failing — guise, toward what an empowering ecclesia might look like, I offer two poems, both with a call to movement, mission, and empowerment. The first poem examines the vision of John the Baptist, popularly known as the precursor for Jesus. However, some scholars (e.g., Sheehan 1986, 57) depict John and Jesus as representatives of two radically different messages requiring on the part of Jesus a transition from one to the other: John's preaching was as riveting as that of Jesus, but different in tone and substance. Whereas John had emphasized the woes of impending judgment, Jesus preached the joy of God's immediate and liberating presence. A dirge had given way to a lyric.

For Jesus this may have been quite a difficult and dislocating move and for the people quite a disturbing and confusing one. In our time of major cultural and spiritual change, we too are likely to be confronted with disturbing — even confusing — changes and transitions that will require a great deal of discernment. Hopefully the reflections of this poem will animate us on our way:

## From Fasting to Feasting

*The Baptist had them trembling with fear of things to come.*
*The ashes and the sackcloth,*
*The penance and the pain,*
*The fearful hand of judgment*
*What merit would they gain?*
*Apocalyptic vision—the frightening doom to come,*
*And the odds are stacked so heavy 'gainst those who would*
    *succumb.*

*Jesus joined the Baptist's rally, exploring future fate.*
*To seek his own vocation,*
*Excitement all around,*
*Awaiting the Messiah*
*The promised hopes abound.*
*But the people feel unworthy and are told they must repent*
*Lest they miss the golden moment of God's Messiah sent.*

*Jesus gazed upon the strategy and the Spirit led elsewhere.*
*He questioned the foundation*
*Of the fasting and the prayer*
*Envisioning alternatives*
*Of a strong prophetic flare.*
*Instead of disempowering those already colonized*
*He dreamt a new companionship with a dream to energize.*

*Jesus left aside the Baptist and chose another way.*
*The penance and the fasting,*
*The desert of the heart,*
*Instead let's dance in feasting*
*Set free and celebrate.*
*The powers were badly shaken, they could not comprehend*
*How people so transformed would throw convention to the*
    *wind.*

*They thought the other prophet was Elijah back once more.*

*The healing and the teaching,*
*Empowering liberty,*
*And the open common table,*
*Transgressing all decree.*
*While stories of empowerment, subversive to the core,*
*Their religion was in tatters with a future so unsure.*

*The attack upon the temple called the long awaited: halt!*
*The Baptist they beheaded,*
*For ethical repute;*
*But 'twas Roman crucifixion*
*Condemning Jesus mute.*
*Yet, companions for empowerment were already on the trail,*
*And the visionary from Magdala made sure it wouldn't fail.*

The second poem describes the challenge of discipleship itself. This is a vastly more complex subject than is generally recognized either in scholarship or in popular preaching. Rather than being an actual historical group, the twelve may be much more a symbolic group representing the patriarchal tradition of the twelve tribes of Israel. Certainly, there were other followers in the Jesus movement, with the possibility that it was the women disciples who played the more crucial role.

We also need to note the context of mutuality: the twelve apostles are sent out in pairs (Mark 6:7), a piece of information that both Matthew (10:5–15) and Luke (9:1–6) either miss or deliberately ignore. Frequently in the Gospels, when the male apostles act in isolation, they tend to get things wrong; despite the guideline in Mark 6:7, we rarely hear of them acting in twos. All of which leads the poet to ask: Are the dynamics of patriarchal power and organization skill preventing Christians from engaging in a more mutual way with the tasks of discipleship?

## Justice for Discipleship

*To the fore are twelve apostles, the Gospels name so clear,*
*Significantly are male beyond dispute.*
*Much attention placed on Peter,*
*Others' roles are so much feebler,*
*With Judas always hailed as traitor.*
*They're not the most exemplary for a call we deem so high!*

*Luke expands the core discipleship to seventy or more,*
*With a strategy to travel forth in pairs.*
*Perhaps sister and a brother,*
*Married couples being another,*
*Martha-Mary moving further.*
*The context for discernment evokes a deeper truth.*

*Luke alone suggests that women played a crucial role as*
         *well,*
*Though his patriarchal bias is all too clear.*
*Subverted to oblivion*
*Is the name of Mary Magdalene;*
*An apostle to the Risen One,*
*Seditiously subverted by the history of power.*

*So discipleship is complex, but evidence subdued,*
*The truth will take some effort to recoup.*
*Companions for empowerment,*
*Includes diverse endowment,*
*Calling justice for a movement*
*That far too long has undermined the true disciple's call.*

*The role the twelve apostles play needs questioning in depth*
*As patriarchal heroes they depict.*
*Oft act in isolation,*
*React in consternation,*
*Rare glimpse of consultation.*
*Not very inspirational for a mission to empower!*

*While the women as we glimpse them in the hour of awful*
*doom*
*Remain steadfast and together in their task.*
*Embracing pain courageously,*
*Discerning truth incisively,*
*They move ahead decisively.*
*They are the ones who set aflame the Christian dream of*
*hope.*

*It's time to rectify the past for justice to prevail*
*And consign our patriarchal bias to doom.*
*Discipleship equality*
*Empowering all with dignity,*
*Proclaim Good News for unity.*
*Companions for empowerment embrace every human*
*being.*

## Radical Relationality

In the opening quotation, Carl Raschke suggests that radical relationality will characterize the churches of the future. Indeed, this
has to be the antidote to the abusive and violent power in which
Christianity has been embedded for centuries. More significantly,
for this book, is the centrality of those right relationships evoked
in the name of the Companionship of Empowerment. What kind
of church — and what ecclesiology — stands the best chance of
honoring the relational empowerment of the new Companionship? Do we need an institutional model? Do we need hierarchical
leaderships? Do we need rituals (sacraments) in which we try
to score points over other religions, and sometimes vie within
the Christian denominations themselves over rituals and rubrics?
And can a church that places such a high premium on the dualism
between the sacred and the secular truly serve the Companionship
of Empowerment?

We can only hope to respond authentically to these questions by asking a more penetrating question: *What model of church did Jesus desire for his perennial dream of the Companionship of Empowerment?* There is no ready or easy answer to this question, because we can't even be sure that Jesus wanted a church, or any officially organized religious movement, in his name. There are strong indications that he desired local empowering communities, of the type St. Paul seems to have developed in his missionary travels. Inevitably, these would be become more formalized as numbers grew and influence expanded. This development in itself does not warrant the top-down institutions that began to emerge in the name of Jesus. In fact, this seems to be where the problem originated: Jesus was viewed as God's regal, imperial representative on earth, and the church became his imperial territory, quickly assuming the power-laden trappings of imperial control and domination. Instead of embracing the vision, we turned the individual person of Jesus into an imperial hero, and in that process we subverted the dream for which that person lived and died, namely, the Companionship of Empowerment. In a word, the Kingdom of the Church displaced the Kingdom of God.

It is difficult after a time-span of two thousand years to reclaim the more authentic foundations of our faith as a Christian people. We need to discern our way through an enormous amount of imperial clutter, with its gross preoccupation on trying to safeguard power, control, and dominance. Second, as indicated in chapter 3 above, we need to confront and discard the imperial understanding of personhood that we imposed upon the historical Jesus (and which we continue to impose upon ourselves) and strive to reclaim the relational understanding, congruent with the egalitarian dynamics of the Companionship. It feels almost like trying to reinvent the church from the ground up, a church that mirrors and serves that vocation to empowerment and liberation which is at the heart of the Christian Gospel.

If we are to allow this relational model of church to unfold, and more importantly if we are to genuinely support its emergence, we face a call to a quality of discernment unknown to previous generations. Ours is a new time as evolution takes us across new thresholds and often toward horizons we would rather not have to embrace. We need an enlarged generic vision for this undertaking, and fortunately we are blessed with resources of our time that can assist us in this task. Sadly, most churches are not in tune with these resources; in many cases they are not even aware of their existence.

## 1. A Cosmic Species

The traditional Christian spirituality of flee the world, turn our backs on the world, and leave its fortunes in the hands of those in the secular sphere has long outlived its relevance and usefulness. Thanks to new developments in science and cosmology we see creation afresh as God's first and enduring revelation for us. Creation itself is our primary sacred space, requiring today all the spiritual and theological wisdom we can bring in order to engage with it in a more transparent and responsible way. For many contemporary Christians the spiritual questions that engagement with today's world begets leaves the church floundering in an ocean of irrelevance. The ecclesiastical cosmic view is narrow, functional, moralistic, and excessively anthropocentric. To many Christians it feels like two totally different worlds, and the church faring as the inferior in almost every sense.

## 2. The Culture of Relationality

One of the more revolutionary insights of the new cosmology is that we live in a relational universe. Everything is programmed to relate. Quantum physics may well be the primary inspiration for this new insight. Gone is the primacy of material objects bouncing off each other like discrete competitive units. Interdependence and relationality characterize the web of life with a dynamic that cannot be mechanically measured nor anthropocentrically controlled. The whole is greater than the sum of the parts. Every person and every structure is called to a new sense of accountability, which relativizes every patriarchal structure including ecclesiastical ones. Egalitarian partnerships are the way forward for everything — and everybody — in our participatory universe.

## 3. The Inspiring Spirit

Millions in today's world are suspicious of religion and weary of its self-serving rhetoric. Correspondingly millions are searching for a new spirituality.[15] Once again, science may be the crucial catalyst at work in this new emergence. We know that energy is the pervasive stuff of the universe. And energy energizes, thanks to the inherent power theologically known as *Spirit* (see Kim 2007; Vondey 2009; Wallace 2005). Living Spirit permeates everything in creation and has done so from time immemorial.

While science still views energy as a random process until we use or channel it, new horizons in theology suggest that the Holy Spirit "inspires" energy into a sense of direction and purpose, with the capacity for relationship as the central dynamic. All energy is geared toward relationships: the theory of entanglement in modern physics (Clegg 2006; Cannato 2010; Winter 2009), interdependence throughout the ecological domain (Primavesi 2003; Suzuki 2002), altruistic cooperation in nonhuman creatures (Margulis 1998; de Waal 2005), empathy as a determining factor in human behavior (Keltner et al. 2010; Rifkin 2009), and the calls for the rehabilitation of relationality in theological endeavor (Keller 2008; Isherwood and Bellchambers 2010). It is from this growing spirit-driven momentum of our time that spirituality evokes a new mystic-type awakening, leaving formal religion looking irrelevant and outdated and leaving the churches floundering and bewildered in their inability to offer a meaningful response.

## 4. Nonviolent Empowerment

Of all the issues confronting humanity today, violence bewilders and bedevils every aspiration for a life of greater meaning and hope. The earth itself is battered and bruised because of exploitation and commoditization. Humans have embraced a planetary trajectory veering headlong toward annihilation. And in our petrified imaginations all we can come up with are more violent strategies to undo the violence that besieges us from every angle.

In the wake of World War II, the United Nations came into being, and its brave prophetic vision has been compromised ever since. The dream behind the United Nations is that of one people inhabiting one earth. All our man-made divisions, including nation-states, are barriers to that one unified humanity. Instead of the highly artificial and contentious units known as "nation-states" we need a reorganization of our planetary well-being using something more organic like the *bioregion* as our basic unit for empowering governance. Otherwise, we may be condemned to continue the cycle of unmitigated violence to an eventual point of total self-destruction. Because of its attachment to the dualistic split between the sacred and the secular, the church often seems paralyzed in its inability to embrace this urgent, global issue of our time.

## 5. Permanently Failing Institutions

The worldwide financial crisis at the end of the opening decade of the twenty-first century made it all too clear that our major institutions of governance, politics, and finance are a great deal more vulnerable than most had suspected. Not alone are they failing us badly, but many suspect they may not even be congruent for the empowering well-being of either humans or the living earth itself. They are archaic and irrelevant, with a covert — sometimes overt — agenda of perpetuating power for its own sake. Driven by fierce competition and capitalistic economics, we evidence today a growing cultural awakening that those institutions that have served us in the past will not be suitable for the future. We will need to co-create alternatives, and with an urgency that is becoming more pressing by the day. The hunger for new companionships of empowerment percolates through the sphere of contemporary life.

### 6. Global Information Networking

Even in the remotest parts of the planet people know of computers, e-mail, and cell phones. Teenagers in very poor parts of Africa, and known to be illiterate (can't read or write), nonetheless are capable of sending text messages, and even e-mails, to friends on other parts of the planet. Social networks like Facebook and Twitter connect peoples across distances and cultures as never before. And the power of information, formerly in the hands of the few, is now accessible to millions. For the first time ever, growing numbers realize that information is power — and can contribute enormously to empowerment of self and others.

No longer can people be fobbed off with patronizing answers in the name of power, politics, or religion. People will question and openly disagree. People are becoming more reflective, discerning, and critical. And as with all major cultural transitions, there is the shadow side, with people becoming voyeuristic, insatiably curious, manipulative, and devious — largely devoid of educational resources to attune people in a more informed way to the positive and negative dimensions of the World Wide Web. Institutional Christianity is only beginning to wake up to the information age, having already lost millions dissatisfied and disillusioned with yesterday's answers to contemporary questions.

## Empowering Ecclesial Communities

An empowering church for the twenty-first century must be able to engage with, and speak intelligibly to, the emerging world of our time. Above I list six features — signs of the times — of the contemporary global landscape. These are among the evolutionary influences of our time, dramatically changing how people think and behave. In all the above developments, the potential for good far outreaches the possible deleterious effects, but this positive potential is unlikely to be realized without an empowering spiritual culture that will both challenge and inspire people in their daily engagement with life.

The prerogative for this spiritual influence currently rests with formal churches and religions, but these are failing dismally to meet contemporary needs. They provide neither meaningful companionship nor authentic empowerment. In this modern complex world, the appeal and relevance of Jesus — and the Christian Gospel — is more than holding its place. In fact, interest in the historical Jesus, culturally and spiritually, prevails across all cultures in the modern world. People, however, do not look to churches in their desire to connect with Jesus. They are more likely to check information online, rather than speak to a pastor or to somebody versatile in matters of Christian faith.

It is not merely the public face of the churches that needs redress. The crisis is internal rather than external. The churches seem to have lost their vitality and raison d'être. I suggest it has disconnected from its more authentic source, which is not allegiance to an imperial Christ, but to that fiery, prophetic, empowering vision of the Companionship of Empowerment, a dangerous and liberating movement, with a power for truth that endures across time and culture.

In theory, a more invigorating church for the future can readily be envisaged. We glimpsed the potential in the global excitement around Basic Christian Communities (BCCs) that surfaced in the closing decades of the twentieth century. BCCs flourished mainly in Central and South America, extending not to the masses, as is often presumed, but to a relatively small sector of the Christian population. However, because the experience was so empowering and the evolution felt so authentic (in terms of the Companionship of Empowerment), the BCC movement sent prophetic vibrations across the entire Christian world. Intuitively, the people of God recognized this movement as the church as it could be — and should be! And not surprisingly, the ecclesiastical authorities felt the threat to their own power and became petrified, defensive, and reactionary.

It is popularly believed that the BCC movement has for the greater part been suppressed and paralyzed by conservative church authority. My sense is that the movement has been driven underground, and as a social scientist I know all too well that what has been driven underground will one day surface afresh and with a cultural vehemence that can no longer be subdued. The situation is very similar to that of the global culture of social networking, largely ignored and frequently domesticated by national governments, but as researchers like Manuel Castells (2000) and Paul Hawken (2007) highlight, it is in all probability one of the most empowering, evolutionary developments of our time.

I suspect the Companionship of Empowerment is one of those archetypal, subliminal forces that no imperial force can suppress or undermine. It will continue to break through and to break out. It is a creative energy of the living Spirit that cannot be subdued. And when it blossoms anew it is likely to materialize as dynamic small groups, akin to the BCCs. When that day comes, then assuredly the church will be born afresh, and Gospel empowerment will once more become, not the reserve of the ecclesiastical few, but the grace of the rank and file, the Body of Christ on earth.

Hopefully the reflections of this book offer something of the fresh hope that millions are yearning for and that it will encourage many, not to be waiting for reform and renewal from on high, but to press forward with bringing about the new companionship of faith invested in empowering communities, promising life and hope for a different future.

Epilogue

# Gospel Empowerment
# Alive in Poetry

*Poetry does not work for everyone, but works for the many who open themselves to it. As the world changes from the long winter into spring, and everything takes on a freshness and a spiritual meaning, just so poetry can quicken, enliven the interior world of the listener.* — MARY OLIVER

*Poets are the unacknowledged legislators of the future.*
— PERCY BYSSHE SHELLEY

The Synoptic Gospels of Matthew, Mark, and Luke frequently allude to the Kingdom of God, translated from the original Greek *Basileia tou Theou*. In both English and Greek, the phrase denotes a God of regal power, in charge of the heavenly Kingdom, and commissioning a regime on earth to perpetuate the same divinely mandated, hierarchical governance. Jesus came to be understood as the primary delegated One for this divine mission — particularly after the appropriation of Constantine in the fourth century.

Even a cursory awareness of church history will indicate that Christianity has never been at ease with Constantine's appropriation, and already in his own lifetime hermits and monks launched a nonimperial counterculture. In our time that desire to reclaim alternative Christian vision has reached a new level of maturation, one enhanced by a fresh understanding of the Aramaic Jesus, among other driving forces. As we have already discussed, in Aramaic, the English and Greek renderings of the "Kingdom of God" explode into a literary genre almost unrecognizable in the other versions. Rational, concise prose gives way to a philological elaboration that requires a very different sense of linguistic engagement. Poetry rather than prose begins to occupy the high ground.

Parables and miracles break open what now translates better as the *Companionship of Empowerment*. As I illustrate throughout the pages of this book, both strategies require a great deal of creative imagination, including verbal articulations that defy and transcend prosaic neatness and concreteness. Parables and miracles are not rational, logical, analytical stories. They defy the criteria of normalcy and stretch the creative imagination toward subversive, revolutionary engagement. They threaten major disruption for a familiar, manageable world, and lure the hearer into a risky enterprise, but one that has promise and hope inscribed in every fiber of the dangerous endeavor.

For some years now, I have been exploring Gospel wisdom through the medium of poetry, some of which is included in the present work. It is both daunting and haunting what Gospel poetry can illuminate. For me, at least, it brings alive the Word of God in totally new ways. And I suspect the full impact of the Companionship of Empowerment will be difficult to access or understand without recourse to the wisdom of the poet.

Consequently, I will conclude this book with some poems confronting, transforming, and re-visioning the dynamics of power being played out in the living context of the Gospel narratives.

## Unmasking the Hidden Idolatry

In the Gospels we encounter anecdotes with what appears to be a counterimperial challenge, usually covert and subtle in nature. For instance the episode about paying tribute to Caesar (Mark 12:13–17) may well have to do with the fact that many Roman coins bore an image of Caesar — not merely to invoke respect for the emperor, but possibly also to highlight his status as one imbued with divine power. The challenge of Jesus' words, therefore, is a counter to imperial idolatry, rather than the sometimes popular interpretation of maintaining a clear distinction between political and religious matters.

A similar intriguing example is that of the reed blowing in the wind (cf. Luke 7:24ff.). N. T. Wright (2004) provides a cryptic explanation for the loaded "postcolonial" question: What did you go out to see?

> When Herod Antipas chose the symbols for his coins, just a few years before the time of Jesus' public ministry, his favorite was a typical Galilean reed. You would see whole beds of them swaying in the breeze by the shores of the sea of Galilee.... "What did you go out to see?" asked Jesus to the crowds who had gone to be baptised by John and were now following him. "A reed swaying in the breeze?" They would have got the message. Were you looking for a new king — another one like old so-and-so up the road? If they missed the point, the next line brought it closer home. Were you looking for someone wearing the latest splendid fashions? If so, you were looking in the wrong place: the royal palace is the place for luxurious clothes. Well, then what were you looking for? A prophet...! To talk about Herod on the one hand, even by implication, and to talk about John on the other, are ways of talking about the figure who stands in between them. (Wright 2004, 86–87)

Is that where every Christian is called to stand? In between, in the liminal space, where we are invited to locate our prophetic presence over against the normalcy of inherited power systems, but also with the consciousness that those same systems must be challenged, critiqued, transformed, and replaced as Jesus eminently demonstrates in the program for the Companionship of Empowerment.

## Denouncing the Royal Reed

*What did you go out to see?*
*A reed shaking in the wind?*
*Swaying to the whimsical mood*
*Of imperial royal demeanor,*
*Impervious to those who seek power to set the people free.*

*What did you go out to seek?*
*Another royal patron,*
*Dressed to the kilt in splendid décor,*
*Wallowing in opulent luxury,*
*Deaf to the cry of all who stand outside the gate.*

*So what did you go out to see?*
*Not a king but a prophet!*
*One who turns the system upside down,*
*Denouncing all that consumes in power*
*While proclaiming hope — oft in the face of desperation.*

*And the one who follows on this way,*
*A prophet I tell you and a great deal more!*
*For the least in God's New Reign,*
*Like the reeds along the lakeside,*
*Dance and flicker to the light of new hope.*

*What Herod had colonized in reed,*
*The seal that stamped his power,*
*The sedge along the water side,*
*Could also catalyze the messianic hour.*

Various forms of idolatry are insinuated in Gospel lore, increasingly the focus of critical scripture study in our time. In chapter 7 above, I highlight the tendency to idolize male hegemony, and, in these concluding reflections, I delineate once more its subtle and pernicious nature. Drawing on research of Durber (1992) and Slee (1984), Corley (2002, 54ff.) highlights a strong andro-centric bias in the parable stories. Of the 104 parables/sayings in Matthew's Gospel, 47 involve human actors, with 85 characters in all. Of the 85, 73 are men and 12 are women, 5 of whom are foolish maidens. In Luke's Gospel, we have 94 parables and sayings comprising 108 human characters; of the 108, 99 are men and 9 are women. These subtle dynamics need to be exposed and confronted if true spiritual empowerment is to be released from within Gospel lore itself, and reclaimed as a central dimension for Christian praxis in our own time.

## Exposing Colonial Rhetoric

*Postcolonial echoes within parabolic lore*
*And the traces are quite subtle and discreet.*
*While the men depict significance,*
*With work and duty in deference,*
*And weather well some tough offense,*
*They know they are in charge.*
*But women cast in passive role,*
*With silly tasks like sweep the floor,*
*Or wasting time one coin restore,*
*Frivolity invoked.*
*There's something out of balance here:*
*We must speak truth to power.*
*And expose corrupting rhetoric*
*If justice is to flower.*

*The postcolonial rhetoric has hist'ry on its side*
*The task of reconstruction will take time.*
*The vestiges well hidden*
*And to scrutiny forbidden*
*With questions we can't quieten*
*Seeking justice for the truth.*
*Equality for gender,*

*Empowerment we must render*
*Exclusions all dismember*
*Outsiders here no more.*
*Companions for empowerment*
*Is the task that lies ahead.*
*The daunting reconstruction*
*Becomes our daily bread.*

## Unmasking Deviant Scapegoating

In allegorizing the parables, God — and Jesus — is often envisaged as a king or a powerful ruler, displaying an exercise of power that is clearly at variance with the Companionship of Empowerment. One of the more vivid and disturbing examples is that of the man without the wedding garment expelled from the wedding feast (Matt. 22:11–14), blatantly contradicting the radical inclusiveness of God's new reign.

The man without the proper garment may have been a beggar or refuge all his life. It is equally possible, however, that he became the victim of deprivation and exclusion. As we can glean from some of the parables about workers in the vineyard, reliable employment was a rare commodity. Many people lost their jobs, finding themselves unable to pay rents and taxes. They ended up living as vagrants, and in cultural and spiritual terms became nobodies. In seeking to reclaim the primacy of the Companionship of Empowerment we must ensure that their voice is heard afresh, and that the splitting into insiders and outsiders is outlawed forever. There is no justification for such exclusions, then or now, in the new Companionship.

### The Royal Scapegoat of a Wedding Feast

*My name is Balthazar of God's own chosen race.*
*I had my days of glory and relished pride of place*
*Till misfortune hit the family and left me in disgrace.*

*Amid the highways and the by-ways I spend the lonely
    hours,*
*A refugee forlorn as the system disempowers.*

*There were rumors of a wedding feast, a mighty banquet
    fete,*
*A king who liked big numbers his repute it might inflate.*
*I was among the motley group invited to partake.*
*I took my place at table as I often did of yore,*
*This time in the garments I had slept the night before.*

*In marched a knightly brigand the guestroom to inspect*
*He said we all were welcome till power games would
    restrict.*
*The pointing finger landed on the one with smelly clothes*
*And given marching orders to the highway and hedgerows.*
*While the odor of the cooking left my belly aching sour.*

*An empire needs its scapegoats in order to survive,*
*And a king can only govern by keeping some outside.*
*There are no wedding garments for fugitives like me;*
*We're lucky to have clothing whatever the decree.*
*Of course, clothing's not the problem when the king asserts
    his power!*

*The wedding feast continued but there were some vacant
    chairs,*
*The empty shells of dominance, the many frightened glares.*
*The scapegoats who were clothed in the garments of the
    poor*
*Resisting the dynamics like prophets long endure*
*Awaiting the feast of God's New Reign — true justice will
    procure.*

Of all the scapegoats in Christian lore, Judas stands out as the most notorious. Nobody seems to have a good word for Judas.

For many people it is inconceivable that God (or Jesus) would have forgiven Judas. It seems that all the twelve betrayed Jesus in the end, Judas — according to popular lore — being the one who did it most explicitly.

Simon Samuel (2007, 129) makes the intriguing observation on the subtle way in which the word "betrayed" is used of both Judas and Pilate in Mark's Gospel. Is this a rhetorical device with postcolonial intent? Judas the traitor (Greek: *paradidous*, 14:14) betrays (14:10; 14:18) Jesus to the Judean authorities. The same verb is used for Pilate in Mark 15:24 (*paredowken*), when he "delivers" Jesus to the Roman authorities.

The suspicious imagination of the poet feels uneasy with the popular portrayal of Judas. The poet knows only too well that every imperial system needs scapegoats to survive and flourish. (The philosopher René Girard makes that abundantly clear.) By keeping the attention focused on an external culprit, the system succeeds in keeping its own deviancy under cover, and successfully projects the blame on to the external scapegoats. *Is Judas the scapegoat par excellence* that helps to get the subversive Jesus out of the way, while leaving off the hook the petrified patriarchs who could no longer endure the invasive empowerment of his radical vision?

## The Parody of Betrayal

*By inflating the hero and condemning the traitor*
*We collude in the game of divisive control.*
*We isolate Judas to personify evil*
*When in fact he's a mirror of imperial rule.*
*He knows all the gimmicks in the devious system,*
*The power of corruption with money to boot.*
*Without the betrayal of ingenious traitors,*
*The system collapses and its power can't refute.*

*The caprice and foibles represented in Judas*
*The other apostles betrayed him as well.*

*They all fled in fear lest they too be tortured*
*Colonized in the grip of imperial swell.*
*In the Gospel of Mark comes the sly intervention*
*With Pilate in panic, a quandary so fierce.*
*The only solution while serving the Empire,*
*Is the act of betrayal to the governing force.*

*The story of Judas, the traitor of legend,*
*The scapegoat supreme in a cult of betrayal.*
*Colonial echoes, the power games we render*
*Must never be seen in their weakness to fail.*
*The parodied Judas, the victim of fortune*
*Exposes deception and the cruel games of power.*
*So peel back the layers of colonial rhetoric*
*And let truth be illumined in our hope to empower.*

## Unmasking Confused Power-brokers

There is a dark side to discipleship that few commentators note; it tends to be totally overlooked (or subverted) in official Christian teaching. The twelve apostles, usually portrayed as the first true disciples, often got tangled in power games and frequently seem to have missed the challenges Jesus was presenting to them. We see this clearly in the request of James and John for places of honor in the life hereafter (Mark 10:35–45).

The evangelists also exhibit confusing and contradictory agendas, most notably in John's Gospel, where Jesus is consistently portrayed as a powerful, divine figurehead — perhaps intended to counter the imperial divinity of the Roman emperor, but in the process undermining Jesus as the empowering animator of the new Companionship. Kathleen Corley (2002, 92) observes that Luke's Jesus spends the bulk of his time lounging around with the rich (not with the poor), and rarely associates with "sinners" directly, unless they are specifically described as previously repentant. The more recent emphasis on Luke as the Gospel for the poor and marginalized "...is primarily a modern scholarly construction" (Corley 2002, 183, n.117).

Such inconsistencies engage the poetic imagination, not to be rationally resolved, but exposed and reframed for a new mode of engagement. Poetry facilitates a process of renaming and reconstruction in order to expose colonial corruption and call forth new possibilities for empowering justice.

## Postcolonial Ambiguity

*Liberty to captives and freedom to the poor,*
*Echoes for a breakthrough, to hope it would endure.*
*Countering the forces the empire values most,*
*With internalized oppression like an archetypal ghost.*
*The portrayal is oft ambiguous, unsure where Jesus stands*
*Or is it the Evangelists who undermine his plans?*
*Did Jesus really compare a woman with a dog?*
*Or is that the Gospel writer in a patriarchal fog?*
*Did Jesus give endorsement that Israel should be first*
*Thus relegating all the rest, a strange oppressive twist?*
*In either case we evidence colonial veneer*
*Disrupting the empowerment God's New Reign did declare.*
*The Lukan Jesus mingles much time among the rich*
*And demands the poor converting submit to what he*
　　　*preach.*
*The inner core consulting is Peter, James, and John,*
*One wonders if the Magdalene was largely left anon!*
*We need to question Holy Writ for justice to procure,*
*Exposing the distortions oft making power secure.*
*Even Jesus must be rescued from the patriarchal trance,*
*As companions for empowerment prophetic'ly advance.*

Of all the powerfully confused personalities in the Gospels, Peter exhibits an amazing mixture of collusion, disruption, and transgression. When the prospect of power is on the horizon, Peter is in hyper mood, but any allusion on the part of Jesus to hardship, suffering, or the Cross leaves Peter wilting with panic and fear. His polar moods are inescapable. Deep beneath the complex, contradictory behaviors, however, we detect a heart of gold, one that genuinely wants to follow and give everything to the cause, but finds it so difficult to rise above the power-mongering that has gripped him for so many years.

At the end, we see a petrified, confused man who wishes he had never known Jesus and denies him forthrightly. Somewhere deep in his being, however, is a suspicion that something may yet transpire that would make his faith in Jesus worthwhile. Contrary to the proverbial Judas, Peter does not give up completely. He hangs on to some semblance of a possible future and wishes that the woman from Magdala was not around.

Because Peter has become so identified with papal power and authority, I suspect we have lost most of his authentic history, one with many pitfalls, but nonetheless a glowing and enduring inspiration for all who struggle with power issues and seek meaningful recognition in an empowering way. The poetic imagination suggests that Peter eventually made the empowering breakthrough, having followed Mary Magdalene and the female disciples through Resurrection trauma and eventually into the nascent Christian community where legend tells us he finally died as a martyr.

The following poem envisages Peter in the courtyard on the threshold of Jesus' imminent death, where Peter — consistent with his previous struggle — makes his famed triple denial, yet lives on to make an eventual breakthrough:

## Peter's Denial: Totally Consistent

*Walking at a distance suspicious of the plot,*
*Peter never came too close to sacred fire.*
*The plot is now unraveling — as the hero of his hopes*
*Disintegrates before his very eyes.*

*This messianic let-down, so vulnerable and weak:*
*"This man I do not recognize at all."*
*Ironic'lly the one time that Peter speaks the truth*
*In the courtyard of destabilizing power.*

*A woman's voice to tantalize, resistance to break down*
*While other probing voices infiltrate.*
*The freezing cold of loneliness disrupts the boundary*
*And Peter ventures deep inside the gate.*
*The warm flames of comfort, he's sought throughout his*
      *life*
*Will once again betray fragility.*
*And the flames unmask the reckoning he no longer can*
      *escape,*
*The darkest hour of Peter's destiny.*

*Consistently, however, he honors what he knows,*
*This is not the God-like hero of his dreams.*
*This archetype of woundedness he always has despised*
*And fakes a meager knowledge what it means.*
*"I do not recognize this man — he cannot be from God,*
*Devoid of all the glory of God's might.*
*The messianic hope I've waited on for years*
*Is nowhere in the evidence you're conjuring tonight."*

*The archetypal rooster sent shivers down his spine*
*And Peter heaved his stomach running wild.*
*In this hour of inner torture the tears flowed down his cheek*
*And he faced the outer darkness so beguiled.*
*The mythic hero's journey he'll once again embrace,*
*And he hopes that his defenses won't deflate.*
*Despite the outer darkness the odds against him stack*
*Redeeming grace will hold him in its stake.*

*Peter stood among the shadows bewildered what to do.*
*He could revert to fishing,*

*But he can't resist the searching,*
*There's a woman at the lurching*
*And she's driving him insane.*
*It will take some years to match her in the Spirit's secret*
  *lure,*
*And reluctantly he'll follow where her wisdom will endure.*

## And Finally, the Poet!

Walter Brueggemann (1989) suggests that poetry succeeds prose, that it is only after we have managed reality with the resources of reason and rationality that poetry begins to surface as the resource needed for the next stage. I am grateful to Walter Brueggemann for alerting me to the catalytic power of poetry to break open new meanings in Gospel wisdom. My perception of the process is somewhat different from what he suggests. Rather than viewing poetry as evolving after prose, I see it as the medium that reconnects the seeker with that which was there from the beginning. Gospel wisdom is poetry in its foundational meaning. It came to be inscribed in prose, mainly under the influence of Greek/Aristotelian philosophy, and is now being reborn in something of its original power and creativity.

Brueggemann is particularly insightful in his employment of the managerial metaphor. Management, meant as control, is certainly a key element in the patriarchal will-to-power. In the contemporary world, a range of gurus from various disciplines strive to discern how to manage reality today. Do we have to abandon all semblance of previous models? What if anything should we hold on to? Can there be continuity, or radical discontinuity? And what models for the future offer the greatest promise? On most of these questions, the jury is still out. However, there is widespread agreement that the institutional, power-based, rationally defined ways of perceiving and operating are not likely to be of much use to us from here on.

To dream new possibilities, we need novel strategies, but much more importantly, we need a reawakening of mind and spirit. This is where the poets come into their own. Poetry can penetrate where rational prose cannot probe. And while poetry can never resolve the dilemmas and contradictions to the satisfaction of either the average evangelical Christian or the academic scholar, it can illuminate at least some of the congealed dynamics that keep us ingrained in the old imperial consciousness. And once the old begins to fall apart, the poet can empower us to hold our nerve while we await the new dawn and that which can empower us afresh. Here hope — Christian and otherwise — is born anew.

# Notes

1. One of the pioneering voices of postcolonialism is the Palestinian-American scholar Edward Said and his 1978 book, *Orientalism*. Some of the major voices and works of postcolonial literature include Salman Rushdie's novel *Midnight's Children* (1981), Chinua Achebe's novel *Things Fall Apart* (1958), Michael Ondaatje's novel *The English Patient* (1992), Frantz Fanon's *The Wretched of the Earth* (1961), Jamaica Kincaid's *A Small Place* (1988), Isabelle Allende's *The House of the Spirits* (1982), J. M. Coetzee's *Waiting for the Barbarians* and *Disgrace* (1990), Derek Walcott's *Omeros* (1990), and Eavan Boland's *Outside History: Selected Poems, 1980–1990*.

2. On an initial reading a strong parallel seems to exist between Luke 10:18 and Isaiah 14:12, depicting the king of Babylon as the morning star that fell from "the heavens." The "heavens" here is a reference to the abode of the stars. This Hebrew word is used in just this sense in Genesis 1:14–16, in the phrase "firmament of the heavens," where God placed the sun, the moon, and the stars. The idea of the king of Babylon being depicted as the morning star that fell from the heavens is an image of loftiness and grandeur being brought low, which is exactly what Isaiah was prophesying against the king of Babylon. So Isaiah 14:12 is a depiction of the king of Babylon's demise, a description couched in the vivid imagery of the brightest star of the heavens falling from its place. Obviously, then, Jesus could not have been referring to Isaiah 14:12 in his comments as recorded in Luke 10:18.

3. In one formidable study, the Italian scripture scholar Ilaria Ramelli (2009) makes a compelling case for revisiting and reclaiming the primacy of the translation: *within*. His insights will be taken up in chapter 6.

4. Several commentators on the Kingdom of God draw attention to the tension between the notion of the Kingdom radically present in the here and now (close to C. H. Dodd's notion of realized eschatology) and still awaiting a fulfillment in the future. "It is hard to explain," writes Jose A. Pagola (2009, 119 n.69), "how Jesus could preach a reign of God only for this life without eschatological expectations." In former times, popular Christianity seemed to favor the emphasis on the future — our true home is in heaven. Today the emphasis has swung significantly toward realizing spiritual transformation through a deeper

commitment to divine creativity in the evolving cosmic creation. I suggest this
tension is best resolved by viewing time as an unfolding process always opera-
tive through the continuum of past-present-future. We need all three dimensions
in our call to be co-creators with a God who never ceases to re-create afresh.

5. Ironically, in the entertainment world gay and lesbian people often
appropriate the term "queer," largely unaware (it would seem) of the internalized oppression being adopted, and the subtle but powerful ways in which
such appropriation feeds a culture of homophobia.

6. "For nothing is hidden [*kryptos*] that will not be disclosed, nor is anything secret that will not become known and come to light" (Luke 8:17; cf.
12:2). Later in the Gospel, when Jesus tells the disciples of the fate that awaits
him in Jerusalem, they are unable to grasp what he is saying, for "what he said
was hidden [*krypto*] from them" (Luke 18:34).

7. The reference to the pigs, infected by the demons and rushing headlong
into the sea, is symbolic material open to several possible interpretations. Some
interpret the anecdote as a parable about breaking the bonds of sin, suggesting
that the pigs served to glorify God by providing tangible evidence to the man and
to the people that the demons had actually left him and that their purpose had
been to destroy him even as they destroyed the pigs. It has also been suggested
that the pigs' destruction was God's way of reprimanding their owners for their
being more interested in their livelihood than in the wretched condition of their
demon-possessed neighbor. The more likely meaning, however, is political rather
than personal or interpersonal. The notion of pigs running headlong like a herd
has never been noted in close observation of pig behavior. We seem to be dealing
with a parable about the unwanted presence of the Roman legions. They, of
course, would not have wanted to be sent out of the country, but many Jews
would have wanted to see them driven into the sea. One wonders if there was
an earlier version of this story in which the theme of driving out the Romans
was the crucial point in this strange anecdote.

8. In *Meeting Jesus Again for the First Time,* Marcus Borg wrote: "Spirit
persons are known cross-culturally. They are people who have vivid and frequent subjective experiences of another level or dimension of reality. These
experiences involve momentary entry into nonordinary states of consciousness and take a number of different forms. Sometimes there is a vivid sense
of momentarily seeing into another layer of reality; these are visionary experiences. Sometimes there is the experience of journeying into that other dimension
of reality; this is the classic experience of the shaman. Sometimes there is a strong
sense of another reality coming upon one, as in the ancient expression 'the Spirit
fell upon me.' Sometimes the experience is of nature or an object within nature

momentarily transfigured by 'the sacred' shining through it.... What all persons who have these experiences share is a strong sense of there being more to reality than the tangible world of our ordinary experience. They share a compelling sense of having experienced something 'real.' They feel strongly that they know something they didn't know before. Their experiences are noetic, involving not simply a feeling of ecstasy, but a knowing. What such persons know is the sacred. Spirit persons are people who experience the sacred frequently and vividly. They mediate the Spirit in various ways. Sometimes they speak the word or the will of God. Sometimes they mediate the power of God in the form of healings and/or exorcisms. Sometimes they function as game finders or rainmakers in hunting-and-gathering and early agricultural societies. Sometimes they become charismatic warriors and military leaders. What they all have in common is that they become funnels or conduits for the power or wisdom of God to enter into this world. Anthropologically speaking, they are delegates of the tribe to another layer of reality, mediators who connect their communities to the Spirit." William Herzog (2005, 12) and John J. Pilch (2005) endorse the idea of Jesus as a shamanic-type healer, as do the spiritual writers Bradford Keeney (2006) and Thomas Moore (2009, 137ff.). Kwok Pui-lan (2000, 79–97) outlines how Asian feminists, especially in Korea, are attracted to this same interpretative device; this and other insights from Asian writers on Jesus as Shaman are outlined by Lisa Isherwood (1999, 110–27).

9. Here the reader needs to keep in mind the impact of background influences especially from the Hellenistic culture. According to Philo, the "soul" in the male is characterized by thoughts that are wise, sound, just, prudent, pious, filled with freedom and boldness, and akin to wisdom, whereas the female tends to be irrational and influenced by bestial passions, fear, sorrow, pleasure, and desire from which ensue incurable weaknesses and indescribable diseases (see sources in King 2003, 195 n.7).

10. Apart from references cited in this chapter, a vast literature on Mary Magdalene is now available. I suggest the following as commended scholarly works: Brock (2002); De Boer (2007); Schaberg (2004).

11. Although the evidence is far from conclusive, I am adopting the popular perception that Jesus was unmarried (as does Pagola 2009, 70–73). This has nothing to do with celibacy as popularly understood today: that people committed to the work of God should, as far as possible, keep themselves free from the allurements and distractions of life, including sex, family, etc. Nor would Jesus have had much time for the notion that sex is a form of contagion that eminently holy people should transcend. The notion of Jesus being married to Mary Magdalene, popularized via Dan Brown's *The Da Vinci Code*, is a view based on minimal evidence, and remains unconvincing for most scholars (see the

informed analysis of Schaberg 2004, 152ff.). My conviction that Jesus probably was unmarried is based on his strong prophetic antipatriarchal stance, whereby he does not collude with those relationships (marital, sexual) that would automatically have cast him in the role of a dominant patriarchal male. He evades or transcends the role as a gesture of prophetic protest.

12.  My critique of the Passion narratives is offered as a counter to those who glorify the death of Jesus as central to human salvation, a conviction that has led to much oppressive suffering and abuse, along with the legitimation of violence and torture of those perceived to be heretical. With those of a postcolonial persuasion, I acknowledge other possible interpretations that view the emphasis on royalty as a satire on Roman imperialism and a prophetic counterculture to it. Postcolonial interpretation is quite a recent development and still unknown even to substantial numbers of Christian scholars. Meanwhile, my intention — and hope — is to unravel and reconstruct the violence-ridden and disempowering redemptive myth that Christians have so naively taken for granted.

13.  During the Roman-Jewish war (66–70 C.E.), bodies were often left on the cross for birds of prey to devour or dumped in a pit for wild animals to eat. It is unlikely that this would have happened to Jesus. However, he was crucified for being a subversive, and a dishonorable burial may have been a consequence. If Jesus' body was salvaged, as all four Gospels indicate (by Joseph of Arimathea — assisted by Nicodemus in John's version), we need to ask if Joseph of Arimathea, being a prominent member of the Council (Mark 15:43), is fulfilling a royal role in the story: if Jesus was a king, surely he would have been buried in a royal manner by an eminent person. As we become clearer on the key role played by women in funerary rites at the time (cf. Corley 2010), we cannot exclude the possibility that the women "watching from a distance"(Mark 15:40) played a crucial role, not merely in the burial of Jesus' body but also possibly in retrieving it in the first place.

14.  The Gospel texts give the impression that the conversion to new hope and life happened for some in a few hours, for others in a few days, over a time span of at most a few weeks. And the process was complete, it seems, in the conferring of the Holy Spirit forty days later. Here, I suggest, we are dealing with sacred (kairos) time and not chronological time. We also know that forty is a sacred number, denoting a long period of time, years rather than days I wish to suggest. Having worked through some of their painful grief, the women were the first to be "resurrected" — some weeks or months after the death of Jesus. I suspect it was many months, possibly years, before most of the male followers came on board.

15.  Today we employ the concept of "spirituality" with a vast range of meanings, many inchoate and contradictory. An evolution is taking place, with a

range of expressions and experiences that seem amorphous and at times bewildering. For a good overview, see Lynch (2007) and King (2008). Heelas and Woodhead (2005) provide a valuable critique of the new age dimensions often associated with modern spirituality, while Carrette and King (2004) provide a valuable (though incomplete) assessment of how spirituality has been co-opted by market forces today.

# Bibliography

Althaus-Reid, Marcella. 2003. *The Queer God*. New York: Routledge.

———, ed. 2006. *Liberation Theology and Sexuality*. Aldershot, Hampshire: Ashgate.

Armstrong, Karen. 1993. *A History of God*. New York: Random House.

Barclay, William, and John Drane. 2001. *The Gospel of Matthew*. The New Daily Study Bible. Vol. 2. Edinburgh: Saint Andrews Press.

Bartlett, Anthony. 2001. *Cross Purposes*. Valley Forge, Pa.: Trinity Press International.

Bauckham, Richard. 2002. *Gospel Women,* Grand Rapids, Mich.: W. B. Eerdmans.

Bhabha, Homi K. 1994. *The Location of Culture*. New York: Routledge.

Blomberg, Craig L. 1986. "The Miracles as Parables." In *Gospel Perspectives*. Vol. 6. Sheffield: JSOT Press, 327–59.

Borg, Marcus. 1994a. *Jesus in Contemporary Scholarship*.Valley Forge, Pa.: Trinity Press International.

———. 1994b. *Meeting Jesus again for the First Time*. San Francisco: HarperOne.

Borg, Marcus, and John D. Crossan. 2009. *The First Paul: Reclaiming the Radical Visionary behind the Church's Conservative Icon*. New York: HarperCollins.

Boulton, David. 2008. *Who on Earth Was Jesus?* Washington, D.C., and Winchester (UK): O Books.

Bourgeault, Cynthia. 2008. *The Wisdom Jesus*. Boston and London: Shambhala.

Brandon, S. G. F. 1967. *Jesus and the Zealots*. New York: Charles Scribner and Sons.

Brock, Ann Graham. 2002. *Mary Magdalene: The First Apostle*. Cambridge, Mass.: Harvard University Press.

Brock, Rita N. 1992. *Journeys by Heart*. New York: Crossroad.

Brock, Rita N., and Rebecca Parker. 2008. *Saving Paradise*. Boston: Beacon Press.

Brueggemann, Walter. 1978. *The Prophetic Imagination*. Minneapolis: Fortress Press.

———. 1986. *The Hopeful Imagination.* Minneapolis: Fortress Press.

———. 1989. *Finally Comes the Poet: Daring Speech for Proclamation.* Minneapolis: Fortress Press.

———. 1993. *The Bible and Postmodern Imagination.* Minneapolis: Augsburg Fortress.

Butler, Judith. 1990. *Gender Trouble.* New York: Routledge.

Bynum, Caroline Walker. 1991. "The Female Body and Religious Practice in the Later Middle Ages." In *Fragmentation and Redemption: Essays of Gender and the Human Body in Medieval Religion.* New York: Zone Books, 181–238.

Cannato, Judy. 2010. *Field of Compassion.* Notre Dame, Ind.: Sorin Books.

Carrette, J., and Richard King. 2004. *Selling Spirituality.* London: Routledge.

Castells, Manuel. 2000. *The Rise of the Network Society.* New York: Wiley-Blackwell.

Clegg, Brian. 2006. *The God Effect: Quantum Entanglement.* New York: St. Martin's Press.

Corley, Kathleen. 2002. *Women and the Historical Jesus.* Santa Rosa, Calif.: Polebridge Press.

———. 2010. *Maranatha: Women's Funerary Rituals and Christian Origins.* Minneapolis: Augsburg Fortress.

Craffert, Pieter. 2008. *The Life of a Galilean Shaman.* Eugene, Ore.: Cascade Books.

Crockett, William. 1989. *Eucharist: Symbol of Transformation.* New York: Pueblo Publishing Co.

Crossan, John Dominic. 1991. *The Historical Jesus.* San Francisco: HarperSanFrancisco.

———. 1992. *In Parables.* Sonoma, Calif.: Polebridge Press.

———. 1997. "Jesus and the Kingdom," In *Jesus at 2000,* ed. Marcus Borg. Boulder, Colo.: Westview Press, 21–53.

———. 1998. *The Birth of Christianity.* San Francisco: HarperSanFrancisco.

———. 2007. *God and Empire.* San Francisco: HarperOne.

Crossan, John Dominic, and Jonathan L. Reed. 2004. *In Search of Paul.* San Francisco: HarperSanFrancisco.

Crossan, John Dominic, and Richard Watts. 1996. *Who Is Jesus?* San Francisco: HarperSanFrancisco.

Davies, Steven. 1995. *Jesus the Healer.* London: SCM Press.

Day, Bill R. 1998. *The Moses Connection in John's Gospel.* New York: Mariner Books.

De Boer, Esther. 2007. *The Mary Magdalene Cover-up: The Sources behind the Myth.* London: Continuum.

de Waal, Frans. 2005. *Our Inner Ape.* New York: Riverhead Books.

Dewey, Joanna. 1997. "Women in the Synoptic Gospels: Seen but Not Heard." *Biblical Theology Bulletin* 27: 53–60.

Dunn, James G. 2003. *Jesus Remembered.* Grand Rapids, Mich.: W. B. Eerdmans.

Durber, Susan. 1992. "The Female Reader of the Parables of the Lost." *Journal for the Study of the New Testament* 45: 59–78.

Fox, Patricia. 2001. *God as Communion.* Collegeville, Minn.: Liturgical Press.

Funk, Robert. 1996. *Honest to Jesus.* San Francisco: HarperSanFrancisco.

Gebara, Ivone. 1999. *Longing for Running Water: Eco-feminism and Liberation.* Minneapolis: Fortress Press.

———. 2002. *Out of the Depths: Women's Experience of Evil and Salvation.* Minneapolis: Fortress Press.

George, Margaret. 2002. *Mary Called Magdalene.* New York: Penguin Books.

Girard, Réne. 1977. *Violence and the Sacred.* Baltimore: Johns Hopkins University Press.

———. 1986. *The Scapegoat.* Baltimore: Johns Hopkins University Press.

———. 2001. *I Saw Satan Fall from Heaven.* Maryknoll, N.Y.: Orbis Books.

Goss, Robert. 1994. *Jesus Acted Up.* New York: HarperCollins.

———. 2007. *Queering Christ.* Cleveland: Pilgrim Press.

Grau, Marion. 2004. *On Divine Economy: Refinancing Redemption.* London: T. & T. Clark.

Gundry, Robert H. 1993. *Mark: A Commentary on His Apology for the Cross.* Grand Rapids, Mich.: Eerdmans.

Hanson, K. C., and Douglas Oakman. 1998. *Palestine in the Time of Jesus.* Minneapolis: Fortress Press.

Harner, Michael. 1980. *The Way of the Shaman.* New York: Bantam Books.

Harpur, Tom. 2004. *The Pagan Christ.* Toronto: Thomas Allen Publishers.

Hathaway, Mark, and Leonardo Boff. 2009. *The Tao of Liberation: Exploring the Ecology of Transformation.* Maryknoll, N.Y.: Orbis Books.

Hawken, Paul. 2007. *Blessed Unrest.* New York: Viking.

Heelas, Paul, and Linda Woodhead. 2005. *The Spiritual Revolution.* Oxford: Wiley/Blackwell.

Heim, Mark. 2006. *Saved from Sacrifice.* Grand Rapids, Mich.: W. B. Eerdmans.

Herzog, William R. 1994. *Parables as Subversive Speech.* Louisville: Westminster John Knox Press.

———. 2000. *Jesus, Justice, and the Reign of God.* Louisville: Westminster John Knox Press.

———. 2005. *Prophet and Teacher: An Introduction to the Historical Jesus.* Louisville: Westminster John Knox Press.

Hill, Jason. 2002. *On Becoming a Cosmopolitan*. Lanham, Md.: Rowman and Littlefield.

———. 2009. *Beyond Blood Identities: Post Humanity in the Twenty-first Century*. Lanham, Md.: Rowman and Littlefield.

Hillman, James. 2004. *Archetypal Psychology*. Putnam, Conn.: Spring Publications.

Hodgson, Peter C. 1989. *God in History*. Nashville: Abingdon Press.

———. 1994. *Winds of the Spirit*. London: SCM Press.

Horsley, Richard A. 2003. *Jesus and Empire*. Minneapolis: Augsburg Fortress.

Hultgren, Arland J. 2000. *The Parables of Jesus*. Grand Rapids, Mich.: W. B. Eerdmans.

Isherwood, Lisa. 1999. *Liberating Christ*. Cleveland: Pilgrim Press.

Isherwood, Lisa, and Elaine Bellchambers. 2010. *Through Us, with Us, in Us: Relational Theologies in the Twenty-First Century*. London: SCM Press.

Isherwood, Lisa, and Kathleen McPhillips. 2008. *Post-Christian Feminisms: A Critical Approach*. Aldershot, Hampshire, and Burlington, Vt.: Ashgate Books.

Jay, Nancy. 1992. *Throughout Your Generations Forever: Sacrifice, Religion, and Paternity*. Chicago: University of Chicago Press.

Jennings, Theodore. 2009. *The Man Jesus Loved*. Cleveland: Pilgrim Press.

Johnson, Elizabeth. 2002. *Truly Our Sister*. New York: Continuum.

———. 2008. *Quest for the Living God*. New York: Continuum.

Jordan, Mark D. 2000. *The Silence of Sodom*. Chicago: University of Chicago Press.

Keck, Leander E. 2000. *Who Is Jesus? History in Perfect Tense*. Columbia: University of South Carolina Press.

Keeney, Bradford. 2006. *Shamanic Christianity*. Rochester, Vt.: Destiny Books.

Keller, Catherine. 2008. *On the Mystery: Discerning Divinity in Process*. Minneapolis: Fortress Press.

Keltner, Dacher, et al., eds. 2010. *The Compassionate Instinct*. New York: W. W. Norton.

Kim, Kirsten. 2007. *The Holy Spirit in the World*. Maryknoll, N.Y.: Orbis Books.

King, Karen L. 2003. *The Gospel of Mary of Magdala*. Santa Rosa, Calif.: Polebridge Press.

King, Ursula. 2008. *The Search for Spirituality*. Norwich (UK): Canterbury Press.

Kraybill, Donald B. 1990. *The Upside Down Kingdom*. Scottdale, Pa.: Herald Press.

Kwok Pui-lan. 2000. *Introducing Asian Feminist Theology.* Maryknoll, N.Y.: Orbis Books.

LaCugna, Catherine. 1991. *God for Us: The Trinity and Christian Life.* San Francisco: HarperSanFrancisco.

Lenski, R. C. H. 1964. *The Interpretation of St. Matthew's Gospel.* Minneapolis: Augsburg.

Liew, Benny. 1999. *Politics of Parousia.* Leiden and Boston: Brill.

Lifton, Robert J. 1999. *The Protean Self.* New York: Basic Books.

Lynch, Gordon. 2007. *The New Spirituality.* London: I. B. Tauris.

Malina, Bruce, ed. 1996. *The Social World of Jesus and the Gospels.* New York: Routledge.

Marcus, Joel. 2006. "Crucifixion as a Parodic Exaltation." *Journal of Biblical Literature* 125, 73–87.

Margulis, Lynn. 1998. *The Symbiotic Universe.* New York: Basic Books.

Mayson, Cedric. 2010. *Why Africa Matters.* Maryknoll, N.Y.: Orbis Books.

Mbiti, John. 1990. *African Religions and Philosophy.* London: Heinemann.

McFague, Sallie. 2000. *Life Abundant.* Minneapolis: Fortress Press.

Meier, John P. 1991; 1994. *A Marginal Jew: Rethinking the Historical Jesus:* Vol. 1: *The Roots of the Problem and the Person;* Vol. 2: *Mentor, Message, and Miracles.* New Haven, Conn.: Yale University Press.

Metz, Johann Baptist. 1980. *Faith in History and Society.* New York: Seabury Press.

Montefiore, Hugh. 2005. *The Miracles of Jesus.* London: SPCK.

Moore, Thomas. 2009. *Writing in the Sand: Jesus, Spirituality, and the Soul of the Gospels.* London: Hay House.

Moxnes, Halvor. 2004. *Putting Jesus in His Place.* Louisville: Westminster John Knox Press.

Neufeld, Dietmar, and Richard DeMaris, eds. 2010. *Understanding the Social World of the New Testament.* London and New York: Routledge.

Newman, Barbara. 1995. *From Virile Woman to WomanChrist.* Philadelphia: University of Pennsylvania Press.

Ogbonnaya, A. O. 1994. *On Communitarian Divinity: An African Interpretation of the Trinity.* New York: Paragon House.

O'Murchu, Diarmuid. 2009. *Jesus in the Power of Poetry.* New York: Crossroad.

———. 2010. *Adult Faith: Growing in Wisdom and Understanding.* Maryknoll, N.Y.: Orbis Books.

Pagels, Elaine. 1995. *The Origin of Satan.* New York: Vintage.

Pagola, Jose A. 2009. *Jesus: A Historical Approximation.* Miami: Convivium Press.

Perkinson, Jim. 1996. "A Canaanitic Word in the Logos of Christ; or The Difference the Syro-Phoenician Woman Makes to Jesus." *Semeia* 75: 61–85.

Pilch, John J. 2000. *Healing in the New Testament.* Minneapolis: Augsburg Fortress.

———. 2005. "Holy Men and Their Sky Journeys." *Biblical Theology Bulletin* 35: 106–11.

———. 2010. "Jesus' Healing Activity: Political Acts?" In *Understanding the Social World of the New Testament.* Ed. Dietmar Neufeld and Richard DeMaris. London and New York: Routledge, 147–55.

Primavesi, Anne. 2003. *Gaia's Gift.* New York: Routledge.

Ramelli, Ilaria. 2009. "Luke 17:21: The Kingdom of God Is Inside You: The Ancient Syriac Versions." *Hugoye: Journal of Syriac Studies* 12: 259–89. See online *http://syrcom.cua.edu/Hugoye/Vol12No2/HV12N2Ramelli.pdf.*

Raschke, Carl. 2008. *GloboChrist.* Ada, Mich.: Baker Academic.

Rifkin, Jeremy. 2009. *The Empathic Civilization.* New York: J. P. Tarcher; Cambridge (UK): Polity Press.

Rohrbaugh, Richard. 2004. *The Social Sciences and New Testament Interpretation.* Peabody, Mass.: Hendrickson Publishers.

Rouselle, Alaine. 1989. *Porneia: On Desire and the Body in Antiquity.* Oxford: Blackwell.

Samuel, Simon. 2007. *A Postcolonial Reading of Mark's Story of Jesus.* Edinburgh: T. & T. Clark.

Sanders, E. P. 1993. *Jesus and Judaism.* Minneapolis: Fortress Press.

Schaberg, Jane. 2004. *The Resurrection of Mary Magdalene.* New York: Continuum.

Schottroff, Luise. 2006. *The Parables of Jesus.* Minneapolis: Fortress Press.

Schüssler Fiorenza, Elisabeth. 1983. *In Memory of Her.* New York: Crossroad.

Segovia, Fernando, and R. S. Sugirtharajah. 2009. *A Postcolonial Commentary on the New Testament Writings.* New York: Continuum and London: T. & T. Clark.

Sheehan, Thomas. 1986. *The First Coming.* New York: Random House. See also online *www.infidels.org/library/modern/thomas_sheehan/firstcoming/.*

Slee, Nicola. 1984. "Parables and Women's Experience." *Modern Churchman* 26: 20–31.

Smith, Adrian B. 2007. *God, Energy, and the Field.* Hampshire (UK): O Books.

Smith, Dennis E. 2003. *From Symposium to Eucharist.* Minneapolis: Fortress Press.

Spurgeon, C. H. 1979. *Spurgeon's Popular Exposition of Matthew.* Grand Rapids, Mich.: Baker.

Sullivan, Nikki. 2003. *A Critical Introduction to Queer Theory.* Edinburgh: Edinburgh University Press.

Suzuki, David. 2002. *The Sacred Balance.* Vancouver: Greystone Books.

Tarlow, Mikela, and Philip Tarlow. 2002. *Digital Aboriginal.* London: Piatkus Books.

Taussig, Hal. 2009. *In the Beginning Was the Meal.* Minneapolis: Augsburg Fortress.

Taylor, Gench, and Francis Taylor. 2004. *Back to the Well: Women's Encounters with Jesus in the Gospels.* Louisville: Westminster John Knox Press.

Taylor, John V. 1972. *The Go-between God.* London: SCM Press.

Taylor, Marc C. 2009. "Refiguring Religion." *Journal of the American Academy of Religion* 77: 105–19.

Tilley, Terence W. 2008. *The Disciples' Jesus.* Maryknoll, N.Y.: Orbis Books.

Vondey, Wolfgang. 2009. "The Holy Spirit in the Physical Universe." *Theological Studies* 70: 3–36.

Wallace, B. Alan. 2007. *Hidden Dimensions: The Unification of Physics and Consciousness.* New York: Columbia University Press.

Wallace, Mark. 2005. *Finding God in the Singing River.* Minneapolis: Augsburg Fortress

Wiebe, Philip H. 2004. *God and Other Spirits.* New York and Oxford: Oxford University Press.

Wink, Walter. 1998. *The Powers That Be: Theology for a New Millennium.* New York: Doubleday.

———. 2002. *The Human Being: Jesus and the Enigma of the Son of Man.* Minneapolis: Augsburg Fortress.

Winter, Miriam T. 2009. *Paradoxology: Spirituality in a Quantum Universe.* Maryknoll, N.Y.: Orbis Books.

Wright, N. T. 1996. *Jesus and the Victory of God.* Minneapolis: Fortress Press.

———. 2004. *Luke for Everyone.* Louisville: Westminster John Knox Press.

## About the Author

Bestselling author **Diarmuid O'Murchu** is a member of the Sacred Heart Missionary Order and a graduate of Trinity College, Dublin. He is a social psychologist whose entire working life has been in social ministry as a couples counselor, bereavement worker, and social worker with homeless people and refugees. As a workshop leader and group facilitator he has worked in Europe, the United States, Canada, Australia, the Philippines, Thailand, India, Peru, and several African countries, facilitating programs on adult faith development.

## Which Diarmuid O'Murchu Book Will You Read Next?

If you are fascinated by science, quarks, black holes, and the way that physics is changing the way we understand our cosmos and ourselves, you'll enjoy reading the bestselling *Quantum Theology: Spiritual Implications of the New Physics*. More than a dialogue between science and religion, this "path-breaking" work (*Values and Visions*) is a bold exploration of divine creativity as seen through the lens of quantum theory, one of the most brilliant advances of our time. This updated version includes reflection questions for groups as well as updates to reflect recent developments in science.

Richard Rohr, author of *The Naked Now*, hails *Catching Up with Jesus: A Gospel Story for Our Time* as "brilliant, liberating, and, most of all, truthful." Building on the insights of *Quantum Theology*, Diarmuid O'Murchu invites us to reconsider the life-changing power of the gospel of Jesus Christ. Imaginative conversations bring us into the life-giving, loving, freeing experience of Jesus, covering themes such as Holy Wisdom, Justice, Miracles, and Radical Inclusiveness.

In *Jesus in the Power of Poetry: A New Voice for Gospel Truth*, Diarmuid O'Murchu uses poetry to retell the gospel stories, where we discover "the sense of awe and wonder, the evocative sense of challenge and shock, the emotional release of affirmation and empowerment" that Jesus offers us all. This new poetic way of encountering Jesus, Mary and Martha, and other major figures in the New Testament teaches us about nonviolence, healing, and solidarity in a way that ordinary prose cannot. As Walter Wink says, "In this book, we encounter another Jesus: the story-teller, the cultural catalyst, the prophetic empowerer, the mystical liberator."

*Quantum Theology* (978-0-8245-2263-6)
*Catching Up with Jesus* (978-0-8245-2298-8)
*Jesus in the Power of Poetry* (978-0-8245-2521-7)

Check your local bookstore for availability.
To order directly from the publisher,
please call 1-800-888-4741 for Customer Service
or visit our website at *www.CrossroadPublishing.com*.